Polishing the Lamp of the Heart

A Devotional

Donn Hutchison

ISBN: 978-0-997-0990-6-5

First Edition

Dedicated to

Rana, Ramzi and Kahlid

Who helped polish the lamp of *my* heart

4

Author's note:

My interest in Islam began many years ago. I was a religion major in college and was headed toward the Methodist ministry. While a student, I attended a Reformed Jewish Temple interested in what Judaism had to say to my spirit. It was during my college days of the early sixties that I became involved with a small Quaker meeting because of its social activism (pro civil rights, anti-Vietnam war). I spent a year as a missionary teacher in a Quaker school nine miles north of Jerusalem. Upon college graduation I returned to that Friends School and even became, for a number of years, the interim pastor of the small Quaker Meeting in Palestine.

Over the years I began to see how Islam is perhaps the continuation of the story that began in the Old Testament and continued in the New Testament. I became conscious of the similarities between these three Great Religions and saw the beauty and wisdom that each one teaches. It is these similarities upon which I have *reflected* in this devotional; based on lines from the Quran, from Sufi writings, and from the poetry of Hafiz and Rumi.

Donn Hutchison

2

4

Polishing the Lamp of the Heart

The call to prayer echoes over the hills and awakens me from slumber. There is something reassuring in hearing the call to the faithful to interrupt the business of the day and the sleep of night. A hundred times a day the remembrance of Allah (God) is on the lips: *may Allah bless your hands; may Allah listen to you; as Allah wants; if it is the will of Allah; may Allah preserve you and give you a hundred years.*

Marriage to a Palestinian Quaker, children, the death of my spouse from cancer, single parenthood, military occupation, two *intifadas* – through all the turmoil that marked my years in Palestine there was always that reassuring call from the mosque.

I began to see that everything that happened was the will of God; that I must submit to His will. Of course there were times when I resisted and bemoaned the fact that things weren't going as I would have them; times when I was troubled with doubt and when my faith was weak, but then a small sign would be there for me to read and I would *see* the presence of God. I would pick up a pine nut still encased in its black shell, and see it as a blessing from God – like the events of our lives, filled with promise of something good. I would find an early flower poking through the thorns and weeds in my garden – a reminder of God. I would watch the sun appear from behind a veil of clouds – and there was God. Wherever I looked He was there!

In the years that I have been studying the Quran, I have seen the similarities between it and the Bible. I have been struck by how, whether Christian or Moslem, we are all the same and that our basic idea of God – of *Allah* –is the same. It doesn't matter if we refer to the Divine as *Allah* or God – (In Islam there are 99 names for God). The Divine is one. He watches over us and cares for us and loves us. Whether Christian, Moslem, or Jew, whatever label we wear, we all learn to submit ourselves to God and trust that what He has planned for our lives is right and good. There will be times when we don't understand, but He is always there. *That* is the reassurance that whispers to my spirit. *That* is the truth of faith.

Through the years I have underlined, highlighted, and marked lines that have *spoken to my condition* (to use a Quaker phrase). It seems right that I share these scraps of wisdom that continue to speak to my spirit and have *polished the lamp of my heart. Inshallah* (God willing), you will find in these words and simple reflections wisdom that will polish the lamp of *your* spirit.

Heaven's Reflection

The task of the Sufi is to polish the mirror of one's self so that one can catch the reflection of heaven during life: unmisted, undistorted, and in all its glory. The Essential Sufism, p.79.

A mirror catches the reflection of what is before it. Decorators recommend placing a mirror in a small room to make the room appear larger as it reflects the opposite, or to place a mirror where it can catch a patch of trees and garden to bring the outdoors in, or to place a mirror where it can dance the morning sun into a room. For a mirror's image to be clear, unmisted, undistorted, it must be polished.

I can remember my mother-in-law instructing me in the proper way of polishing an aluminum pan: steel wool, homemade soap from Nablus, and lots of elbow grease. She would say: *Polish it so it is like a mirror.* After it was polished to mirror-like perfection, it was rinsed and placed in the sun to dry, she said: *so it can catch a bit of heaven.*

We *polish* are souls with words of kindness, with courteous phrases, with acts of thoughtfulness and generosity; smiling at those we wait on, or work with, or pass in the street; letting someone in a hurry step in line before us; making space for a car trying to get into busy traffic; conveniently looking past the small, lingering hurts. It isn't just reading a devotional book, or holy script, or praying, or attending services at the mosque, temple, or church. It is the daily little acts– like having someone in for a cup of coffee and piece of pie- that can keep the mirror of one's self polished so the image it reflects is unmisted, undistorted- a *bit of heaven in all its glory.*

Inshallah (God willing), the mirror of your self will reflect a bit of heaven today.

Obeying Impulses

And if anyone obeys his own impulse to Good, be sure that
Allah is He who recognizes and knows. Sura II: 158

The impulse should be to do good. Once we are sure of this we must obey it without hesitation, whatever people may say. How often do we hesitate to do the impulsive for fear it will be misunderstood, or be seen as intrusive; reluctant because of how it might be viewed. We are taught to be reserved and to control our impulses – but then there are strawberry pies.

In my years as a single father, in addition to baking dozens of cookies, and sweet rolls, and making birthday cakes in the shapes of *Raggedy Anne* and *Superman,* I became quite a good baker of pies – especially *strawberry pies.* I had a student in an 11th grade English class. The moment he walked in the door that first morning of a new academic year it was an epiphany. I had *known* this kid forever! Of course, I hadn't. I didn't even know his name.

In the course of the year, I found out he liked *strawberry pies.* On impulse, I baked two, put them in a straw basket – reminiscent of *Little Red Riding Hood* – and went out to his village early before he and his family were up. I left the basket of strawberry pies on the doorstep with a note on top of the linen napkin covering the pies. On the bus ride home I thought, *"How stupid was that. You didn't even ring the bell!"*

It was pure impulse. If I had been rational about it, it would never have happened. Allah works in mysterious, *impulsive* ways. It has been over a dozen years since I left that basket of strawberry pies on the doorstep. That young man who walked into my 11th grade English class is now a husband and father – and has become, in my heart, as another one of my children, and as dearly loved as they are. It all started with strawberry pies, and *obeying the impulse to do good.*

Sometimes, doing the impulsive act of kindness is Allah's way of touching those around us.

Wisdom of the Heart

There is a wisdom of the heart far different than the wisdom of the head...the wise heart sees beyond outer forms to inner reality. Essential Sufism

Wisdom of the heart? We are taught to use our heads, to think with our minds, to avoid the unrealistic, rather *poetic* notion of the heart being wise. Yet, it is those very things that touch the heart that have the most power in our lives. Our hearts seem to have the power to *see* beyond the outer reality. I can remember hearing the comment as a child: *Now, there is a face that only a mother could love.* The wisdom of the heart. One of my aunts, tall, and willowy, with chestnut hair and dark, doe-like eyes, married a man who only stood five feet in his stocking feet, had large ears that stood out wing-like from his head, and had a face which looked as though it had been formed from misshapen clay. They were married for close to sixty years, had four beautiful children, and were immensely happy. The *wisdom of her heart* allowed her to see how truly handsome he was - to see beyond the outer form to his *inner reality.*

There is an *inner reality* that the heart recognizes. So many unexplainable events are in each of our lives- situations we may have avoided had we looked at the outer form only. Yet, sometimes our *heart sees beyond the outer forms to the inner reality* and we are blessed.

8

Listen to your heart as it whispers to your soul and wisely leads you to things that will bless you and those around you.

Footprints of the Camel

A Bedouin was once asked how he could believe so strongly in a God he could not see. The man replied: 'If you see the tracks of a camel in the desert, do you have to wait to see the camel itself before believing it exists? Essential Sufism (p.74)

The tracks of a camel in the desert are positive proof of its existence. We don't question that a camel has passed that way – there are the tracks! We don't question that it exists –there are its footprints in the sand. How many countless *footprints* do we see every day that witness to the existence of God: the gentle pinks and blues as the day awakens at dawn; the vibrant reds and yellows as the day slips into the darkness of sleep; the tender shoots that push aside the soil as they reach slender fingers toward the sun; a baby's finger grasping your thumb, a seed planted in the earth growing to a mighty tree; a wild poppy among the thorns - all positive proof of the existence of God. We don't have to actually *see* God to believe that He exists – we see the proof of His existence everywhere.

God's footprints are everywhere we look; we can hear the whisper of His voice in the breeze which makes the trees dance; we can feel the warmth of His touch in the sun, and in the arms of those we love and who love us. God is everywhere!

The Night Visitant

And by the sky and Night-Visitant; and what will explain to you what the Night-Visitant is? It is the star of piercing brightness; there is no soul but has a protector over it. Sura 86:1-3

In each of our lives there are times when the night seems dark and foreboding. Times when we close our eyes and wish for sleep but are kept awake by the darkness that seems to penetrate into our souls and casts a veil of doubt and fear over our minds and spirits; times of almost utter despair.

In the months after my wife's death I lay sleepless many nights wrapped in the darkness – the darkness of night, the darkness of spirit, the darkness of despair. There was no way I would be able to cope with caring for a child in third grade and a child in kindergarten; there was no way I would be able to juggle being the traditional *mom at home;* cooking, cleaning, washing, packing lunches, supervising homework, being the nurturer, and being the *traditional dad at work.* There was no way that I could be both *mom and dad*! Even the days – at times – seemed like darkest night.

One evening, after the children were in bed, the kitchen was clean, the lunches were packed and in the refrigerator with a note tucked into each bag reading: *I love you,* I was hanging the wash on the lines on the veranda. As I pegged the clothes to one line, I glanced up at the night-time sky and there was the *wishing star: star light, star bright, first star I see tonight; wish I may, wish I might, have the wish I wish tonight.* And I remember wishing to be loving and strong enough to be both mom and dad to my children. It was at that moment that I realized that even the darkest nights are penetrated with stars of piercing brightness- that I, that *we*, would be all right; that there was *Someone* watching over us, protecting us, guiding us, loving us.

We are *never* alone- even in the darkest night- there is the *Night-Visitant-* the star of piercing brightness that dispels the dark.

Through the darkest night comes the penetrating light of a glorious star. Wait with gentle patience for Allah's decisions. (The Holy Quran, p. 1718)

12

Entering Paradise

*Take all my good deeds. It is enough for me if **you** enter paradise. Sheikh Muzuffer,* Essential Sufism, *p. 134.*

A premise of Islam, as I understand it, is that *all* of our deeds are meticulously recorded and the weight of the good against the bad determines whether or not we enter paradise; that even the smallest deed of goodness, though it be the size of that proverbial *mustard seed,* is written in the book of accounts; that there is complete fairness and exactness in the record keeping; that our term on earth is a probationary period - a chance for us to *do good -* the ultimate reward being: *paradise* where *rivers flow and there is abundant fruit and peace.* What better image of paradise for a people living in a dry, arid desert often rife with fighting than a heavenly oasis where there is water and fruit and peace?

Who would not wish for such a paradise? Who would not wish to do good deeds when one thus could enter heaven? What strikes me about the line of Sheikh Muzuffer is his *willingness* to give all his good deeds to another so he\she could enter paradise; sacrificing his own entrance to heaven and perhaps condemning himself to hell! I am struck by the undeniable love: *it is enough for me if you enter paradise.*

Which one of us, if we thought the balance of our loved one's deeds were too light for his/her entrance into heaven, would not willingly say: *Take all my good deeds. It is enough for me if you enter paradise.*

Whatever our concept of heaven and hell; whether it is a beautiful garden where rivers flow versus a pit of fire where we continually thirst or whether it is nearness to God as opposed to estrangement from God- and whatever our concept of how we enter heaven or are assigned to hell; whether it is based on a record of good and bad deeds, or through belief in atonement- we would want those we love to be in paradise.

Perhaps the love we learn from God would prompt us to say: *Take all my good deeds. It is enough for me if **you** enter paradise.*

Faith is the Knowledge of the Heart

Faith is the knowledge of the heart, the words of the tongue, and the actions of the body. <u>Essential Sufism</u>, p. 88

There are many ways of *knowing*: we know things that we learn through experience; we know things that we are taught and on which we are tested; we know things that can be seen and proven; we tend to feel that knowledge is a matter for the mind, not the heart

Knowledge of the heart is *faith.* There are things that we *know* in our heart that cannot necessarily be proven or taught or learned yet are nonetheless as real as those things that our mind knows. We *know* that we love and that we are loved; we *know* that there is a Power that values us and cares for us and guides us and loves us; we *know* that this current life is not all there is; we *know* there is a heaven. Our hearts know these things. This is faith.

Faith is demonstrated by *the words of the tongue, and the actions of the body.* It is our *knowledge* that we are loved and love that governs the words that we say– how we speak to those we love and value and care about– how we speak to those with whom we come in contact: the people we wait on, the people we serve, our co-workers, the person at the check-out counter, those who serve us, the neighbor, everyone we meet. It is this knowledge – this faith in Allah/God – that should govern *the actions of our bodies;* a firm handshake; the hugs we give our children, our spouse, our parents, our siblings, our friends; the smile; the helping hand; the sympathetic eye contact; going out of our way for someone else - there are so many *actions of the body* that bear witness to what we believe– to our *faith.*

Faith is the knowledge of the heart, the words of the tongue, and the actions of the body. Today, I pray the words of my tongue and the actions of my body will speak of the knowledge of my heart- my faith.

Trays of Light

Prayers for the dead are on the same footing as gifts for the living. The angel goes in to the dead with a tray of light, bearing a cloth of light, and says, "This is a gift for you from your brother so-and-so, from your relative so-and so." And he delights in it just as a living person rejoices in a gift. Al-Ghazzali <u>Essential Sufism,</u> *p. 187*

A nighttime ritual when my children were little was listening to their prayers. We would cuddle together and read each night after their baths - even long after they could read on their own. After reading together each one would go to bed and I would tuck them in. I would bend down and put my arms around them and whisper their bedtime prayer in their ear. The prayer always ended with: *And God bless Mama and Baba and Tata and Sido and Grandma and Grandpa and all the people in the world.* At the time their grandfather and mother were already dead, but, in a real sense, still part of their lives.

I had pictures of their mother all over the house, even on the refrigerator door (I still do and she has been dead almost thirty years). We would tell stories about her, talk about her as though she was just in the next room. We always remembered her. I wanted my children to *know* that death was not the end; I wanted them to know that the *loving* continues.

My wife is buried in another country but in the same town where my married daughter now lives. My daughter is good about tending her mother's grave especially on Mother's Day and the anniversaries of her mother's birthday and death when she takes flowers. When my oldest son got engaged, he took his wife-to-be to the gravesite as his mother was still part of his life. He lives in another state, but whenever he is visiting his sister, he stops to visit his mother's grave and takes a bouquet of flowers - a *gift of a tray of light.*

Our prayers and remembrances of the dead *are on the same footing as gifts for the living.* An angel goes in to them with a *tray of light* and they rejoice.

Remembrance Polishes the Heart

God has made a polish for everything that tarnishes. And the polish for the heart is remembrance. <u>Essential Sufism</u>, p. 17

My home is filled with the previously used bits and pieces of a dozen or more of my wife's relatives. The dining room set is not really a set; the table belonged to one aunt, the chairs to another aunt, the table cloth to another aunt, the hideous ebony bowl with its ivory handle to another aunt, the small sideboard to yet *another* aunt. I like having these *remembrances* of these remarkable, yet ordinary, women around.

On the sideboard, and climbing up the wall behind it, is a garden of framed photos of some of these relatives. I look at these photos as I dust and think about the lives these women lived: One was a grandmother who was widowed very young and left with six children at a time when few women worked outside the house. She turned her home into a boarding house and did cooking and sewing for people. Life was not as she had envisioned it would be, but she managed. One was an aunt who was married at thirteen to an uncle who was thirty-three. She was widowed at eighteen and left with two young children. She couldn't read or write, but she managed. Another photo is of an aunt married in 1926. She soberly looks out into the camera. Her marriage was not that proverbial *match made in heaven,* but she managed.

Some of these women I knew. Some I only knew through stories. What I remember most is their *humor,* their acceptance of what often would appear to be the unacceptable, their ability to *manage,* and their deep *faith* that everything would work out. Their spirits seemed to *shine* as though they had used their experiences as a *polish for their hearts.* These experiences made them *tender* and *sensitive* and *understanding.* They didn't compare, or complain, or bemoan the situation, but they made the best of it. They used the ashes of their dreams as an abrasive to *polish* their hearts. Their spirits shone!

I remember their lives as I live among their things. I remember that even when terrible things happen we are *given the strength to manage;* that Allah truly has made a polish for everything that might tarnish; that even the heart that might tarnish is polished by remembrance that we are never alone– that we will be able to cope- to manage.

God has made a polish for everything that tarnishes. And the polish for the heart is remembrance.

Being Precious in God's Sight

You are more precious than both heaven and earth; you know not your own worth. Sell not yourself at little price being so precious in Allah's sight. Rumi

The call to prayer echoes through the breeze this pre-dawn morning calling the faithful to prayer, carrying praises of God to the receptive ear, reminding me of the preciousness of my children, my grandchildren; the preciousness of family and friends and those I meet in the street.

Almost every morning when I walk to school I pass the same street sweeper. He is a man probably in his forties and walks as though the hinges on his knees were put on backwards. He uses the handle of the dustbin cart he pushes for balance at times. He seems meticulous when he sweeps up the litter in the streets. Every morning when I pass him, I whisper a prayer that *his morning will be blessed.* He is precious in Allah's sight.

Yesterday on my walk to school, for a brief moment, I glanced at a man who wore the brand of a birthmark on half his face. I thought about the struggles he daily faces because of the way he looks. I whispered a prayed that *his day would be blessed.* He probably finds it hard to believe that he is precious in Allah's sight.

I have a granddaughter who will be having her first birthday tomorrow, *inshallah.* She is a bundle of smiles crowned with a mop of curly, curly hair...*more precious than both heaven and earth* to her parents and grandparents and uncles and aunts. It is easy to see how precious she is in Allah's sight.

It is sometimes hard to believe in our personal worth- and sometimes we resign ourselves to being less than what we could be– *we sell ourselves at little price.* We can't believe that we, with our flaws and frailties are precious in Allah's sight. It is easy to see how some could be Allah's precious treasure, but us?

Today, as you go about your tasks, remember: *You are more precious than both heaven and earth;* you have worth in the eyes of God *being so precious in His sight.* Remember that the people you encounter at work, in the store, on the street, in the cars waiting for the light to change are *precious in Allah's sight.* He loves them as He loves you.

Giving Anonymously

A high level of generosity is to give anonymously. <u>Essential Sufism,</u> *p.185 Spend from what Allah has given you. Do not fear poverty. Allah will give you what He has promised, whether you or everyone asks for it or does not ask for it. No one who has been generous has ever perished in destitution. Ibn Arabi,* <u>Essential Sufism,</u> *p. 189*

For many years I had a friend who used me as a go-between for his generosity. He would learn of bright students who had considerable promise, considerable potential, and he saw helping them with their education a good investment– a good return on his money. He gave a relatively modest amount. There were no strings attached or implied, there was only one condition: *the recipient of his gift was never to know the name of the benefactor.* I knew why he had placed this stipulation. He didn't want the students to feel obligated in any way. In the years I have been his go-between I have never betrayed his name to anyone. The Quran teaches that *a high level of generosity is to give anonymously.*

Ibn Arabi suggests that we *give from what Allah has given to us.* Everything we have is really on *loan.* Our lives are blessed by God with whatever resources we have. Our funds are really His funds to be used wisely and generously.

Many years ago I was selling the household items of an aunt after her death. A man and his wife and children came to look over the items. They were in dire poverty. They had lost their home and all their furnishings and were living in two rented rooms. As they looked over the items trying to decide how to use their meager funds, I took the man aside and told him: *My aunt would be so pleased if you took whatever you need.* They loaded up the bed of their pickup truck. I heard his wife say to him that she wished there had been a single bed and some cooking pots. I told him: *You'd really be doing me a favor if you took a bed I have wanted to get rid of. It isn't much to look at, but is too good to just throw away, and I have no place to store it. I have just moved into my in-law's furnished house. I had pots and pans and my mother-in-law had pots and pans. If you could use them, do take the extra set. You'd really be doing me a favor.*

Allah provides for our every need. In the Bible it says: *the birds neither toil nor spin yet God provides for them, how much more will He provide for you.* The same message is in the Quran. *Spend from what Allah has given you.*

Being Content

I am a wealthy man because I am content with whatever God sends me. Sheikh Muzaffer, <u>Essential Sufism,</u> p. 69

I have never made much money, statistically, I am probably well below the poverty line in the West, and would yet be considered quite wealthy in parts of the developing world. It is all a matter of where one's tent is pitched.

When my children were little I used to tell them: *I have all the money in the world – we are really quite well-to-do-* and I suppose, as young as they were, they believed me. I would joke with them that I had *piles of dollars* beneath a loose floor tile in the back room. (There *was* a loose tile in the back bedroom and I would joke with the kids that the pile of money was so high that the tile didn't rest evenly.) If we really thought we needed something, I would say to the kids, somewhat reluctantly, *Well, I could write a check?* Then we would decide it would be so much better to save and *pay cash.*

I *was* a wealthy man because I was *content* to make-do. I bought cheap fabric from a place that sold remnants by weight and made curtains, sheets, pillowcases, and aprons, clothes for Barbie and stuffed animals. I bought the kids underwear and pajamas from boxes the merchant had on the street in front of his shop. I found looking into dustbins compulsive --- who knew what treasures someone had thrown away. I would find a *treasure* and think: *Allah knew I'd be passing by this way.* I *was* wealthy because I was *content* with whatever God sent me. Once a visitor, looking through the rooms of my home, asked where I had acquired a particular lithograph ---*the dustbin;* where I had gotten the antique birdcage hanging in the veranda -- *the dustbin;* where I had purchased the brass planter --*the dustbin.*

Our wealth is measured perhaps in not what we have, but in terms of *what we don't need.*

In my seven plus decades, I realize that I have always had enough; that Allah has always taken care of me; that He has always sent me what I have really needed. I am certainly not wealthy in the definition that some may have of wealth – but *I am a wealthy man because I am content with whatever God sends me.*

Today I am going to be content in the knowledge that whatever God sends me is enough – in fact *it is just right!*

If your words are truthful, if you are good tempered, if you are moderate in taking food, and if you are trustworthy, then you are rich and should not regret the possessions that you may not have. (Essential Sufism- p. 88)

Paradise, because of an Ant

Her friends asked her if she had gone to Paradise because of all her wonderful charities, and she replied, 'I am in Paradise, but it is not because of those charities. It is for the sake of an ant.' Essential Sufism, *p. 218. Service without love is like a beautiful corpse. The outer form is lovely, but it is lifeless.* Essential Sufism, p. 217

I like the story told about the mother of one of the Ottoman-Turk sultans. She was a lady well known for her charitable work. She had built mosques and hospitals and public wells. One day, she was visiting the site of the construction of a hospital, so the story goes. She saw an ant had fallen into the wet cement. She lifted the ant out and set it on its legs. Many years later she died. One evening she appeared in the dreams of several friends. She appeared to be full of joy. When asked if she was in Paradise because of her good works, she gave this famous reply: *I am in Paradise for the sake of an ant.*

It is a reminder that even the lowly ant is part of Allah's creation and therefore of importance. Her kind gesture to so insignificant a thing as an ant got her into Paradise! For years, on seeing a beetle on its back, with its spidery legs pumping in the air, I would *turn it over* thinking: *It too is one of God's creatures.* (Probably in the attic of my mind was a memory of this story!)

Service without love is like a beautiful corpse. The outer form is lovely, but it is lifeless. I have a friend/acquaintance who lives in a nursing home. Every Monday she makes the journey to town, sleeps over in her house, and calls me Tuesday morning to carry her shopping bags to the bus so she can go back to the nursing home. She hates living there and makes these weekly visits to her home on the pretext of *buying food* to prevent starvation at the nursing home! Every Tuesday it is the same conversation on the phone: she asks me if I will come and walk her to the bus; she tells me that I am an *angel* for helping her; I agree to go.

I do go, but reluctantly. I have to take an aspirin before seeing her to prevent the headache being around her causes. I do provide a service --- but in many ways I am like that *corpse* – outwardly the *form* of patience and kindness --- but inwardly the attitude of my service is anything but angelic.

Sometimes we may give service, but with the wrong attitude; we may appear charitable and generous, but on the inside are not!

I would hope that today my service would be filled with love, and like the Sultan's mother from the story, be allowed into Paradise *for the sake of an ant.*

Divine Breezes

Divine breezes from your Lord waft through the days of your life. Listen! Be aware of them. Hadith: Words of the Prophet, Essential Sufism, p. 87

This morning a cool breeze blows through the house pushing the curtains as a wind pushes against the sails. The breeze is perfumed with the fragrance of lavender and Jasmine and *Louisa.* After the horrendous heat of two weeks, this overcast morning with its cool breezes is a welcome gift from God. Just before dawn the call to prayer from the mosque was carried on the wind; now the church bells ring through the breeze reminding the faithful of God.

Sometimes, if the wind is especially strong, we can *hear* it as it makes the branches and flowers sway and dance, and the wind chime sing: refreshing, cleansing, beautiful, a reminder of the Divine.

Divine breezes from your Lord waft through the days of your life. Listen! Be aware! I still hang the wash on clotheslines outside. I like shaking the wet clothes out, pinning them to the line, (in order!) allowing them to be buffeted by the breezes and kissed by the sun. I am thankful for this activity. As I think back through the many years I have hung the wash, I am aware of how soothing to my spirit this mundane activity has always been. It has always given me moments to contemplate other things as my hand mechanically picks up the wet garment, (clothespin in my mouth) and pegs it to the line where it can *dance.*

My father felt that, as long as he had children at home, my mother should not have to scrub floors, wash windows, sweep or dust. At an early age I learned how to keep house. My mother, literally, put on white gloves to check window sills and chair rungs. I can still hear her voice reminding me to sweep behind the door and under the couch because: *God sees even though no one else can.* A simplistic view of a Divine Spirit who is concerned about dust balls behind the door. The truth of the belief that God is everywhere and aware of everything is the importance of her words...one of those *divine breezes wafting through the days of my childhood.*

The phone rings and it is an unexpected call from one of my children just to touch base: one of those *Divine breezes.* I open an email and there is a short note: *Just wanted you to know I love you:* one of those Divine breezes. Pictures of my grandchildren appear on the screen: one of those Divine breezes. I clean weeds from the garden, and there among them is a vibrant wild flower: one of those Divine breezes. A stray dog has dug a trench on the other side of the stone wall, and there beneath her matted fur are four perfect balls of puppy: one of those Divine breezes.

Divine breezes from God flow through the days of our life. We need but feel them –*listen* –be aware. Today I am going to hear, and feel and thus be aware of the Divine breezes that flow through my day.

The Paths to God

The ways to God are as many as there are created beings. But the shortest and easiest is to serve others, not to bother others, and to make others happy. Abu Said, Essential Sufism, p. 198

The ways to God are as many as there are created beings. My maternal grandmother was a Christian Scientist and never took a pill or went to a doctor; my father's mother was a Free Methodist and usually wore long skirts and dresses with sleeves; my parents, in the early years of their marriage belonged to The Church of God and neither smoked, drank, played cards or danced; I was a pre-ministerial student in college thinking of becoming a Methodist minister; I worked in a Friends Boarding School in Palestine, and became a Quaker; (it was there that I became aware of the beauty of Islam) I have a sister who is a Missouri Synod Lutheran, a nephew who is Catholic, and a father-in-law who was Greek Orthodox- you name it, it was in the family pie. Thankfully, *there are so many paths to God!*

But the shortest and easiest is to serve others, not to bother others, and to make others happy. When my children got married I prayed, and continue to pray, that they would make their spouses happy. I would tell them to write a little note saying: *I love you* and slip it into a purse or pocket, lay it on the dashboard of the car, or put it under their spouse's pillow...find little ways to remind your spouse of how much you love her/him. Go to the rock concert he likes; take her out to her favorite Japanese restaurant; watch the kids so she can have a girls-night out; think of ways to make the other know they are loved…that your priority in marriage is to find ways to serve the other…to make your spouse and your children happy. When we serve others, when we make them happy, often we also are happy, and our path is leading us to God.

Not to bother others: I never call to let people know that I am going to stop in for a visit. This has often resulted in my traveling a half hour by bus, only to arrive at the door and find no one home. I don't phone ahead as I don't want to *bother anyone.* My thinking is if I ask to come, then they will have to change their plans, stay home, be sure they have something to serve, be inconvenienced (stupid I know). I figure if I just drop in, I can see if they are on their way out, see if they are in the middle of something, see if it is inconvenient, and stay ten minutes, drink a cup of coffee and go. I often hesitate to phone for the same reason: maybe they are napping; maybe they are bathing the children; maybe they are working in the garden; maybe they are watching a game, in the middle of a movie. I don't want to *bother others.* (I take it to extremes, I know.) Perhaps the real significance of the phrase is to *think of the other* and not so much of one's self.

The ways to God are as many as there are created beings. But the shortest and easiest is to serve others, not to bother others, and to make others happy.

Today, I will find ways to serve others and to make them happy.

Patience: One of God's ninety-nine names

Patience is one of the Ninety-nine names of Divine attributes mentioned in the Quran. It is said that patience is half of faith. If we are impatient, we are no longer in the present; we are busy wishing for a future that has not yet come.
Essential Sufism, p. 183

I have an old-fashioned, hand-cranked sewing machine that belonged to my mother-in-law. It is probably close to ninety years old and still sews a straight stitch. There have been times when – with my bifocals – I can't seem to get the thread into the eye of the needle. I cut the thread yet again, wet it with spit, and with bifocals on the table attempt to once more get the thread into the needle's eye. It may take several times, and mumbled words of encouragement to the machine, before the needle is threaded, only to have the tension not right, and the thread to break. I fiddle and fume a bit before finally getting the machine to work as it did ninety years before. It takes patience.

Sixteen years ago I had brain surgery for a congenital *hole in my head* (my children said that *explained a lot)*. After the surgery the prognosis was that I would never have complete use of my right hand, I would never have fine motor skills, and I would never speak clearly. Gone were the days of playing the piano, knitting sweaters for the kids, and teaching speech. I would walk with a cane, awkwardly use my right hand, and have to repeat words – especially those beginning with 's'.

I didn't count on my sister's tyrannical determination. She *forced* me to play the piano for a half hour each day- my left hand making the chords, my right hand flopping on the keys. She *forced* me to copy articles from the newspaper with my right hand– scrawling out the words like a child first learning to write. She *forced* me to knit dishcloths using big needles and thick cotton. She *forced* me to walk around and around and around her drive waving my arm. She *forced* me to walk around the lake, slowly, leaning on my cane. I hated it.

But within a month I once again could play the piano with both hands; I once again had fine penmanship with the right hand; I once again could follow intricate patterns (leading me to joke that brain surgery improved one's knitting); I could walk without a cane and my speech impediment disappeared. *Patience is half of faith.* I was impatient, bemoaning the loss, envisioning a severely altered future, not living in the present. My sister had faith that with persistence I would recover. *Subhan Allah* (praise God), I did.

It is so easy to get impatient– to want things done *yesterday.* It is hard to wait; sometimes hard to live in the now. I tell my children, when they sometimes wish that things were immediately different: *All in God's good time.* I truly believe that. I am proof of that. Allah loves us and cares for us, and values us, and gives us what we need *all in His good time.*

Today I will be patient; I will live in the moment; I will work, yes, and sometimes try and try again until I can get it just right, but then wait for *God's good time.*

34

Everything is infused with God

*What is **not** God? Everything is infused with God.* <u>Essential Sufism,</u> p. 227

He is there in the call to prayer as it floats through the branches of the trees and slips into my dreams. He is there in the ringing of the church bells rivaling the noise of car horns and the traffic speeding through the street. He is there in the potted plants reaching slender fingers toward the watering can- roots waiting to quench their thirst. He is there in the tomatoes ripe on the vine, the berries plump with sun. He is there in a baby's smile, bright with six new teeth, reaching up chubby arms to be lifted up and carried. He is there in the regimented row of ants, marching with single-minded precision, burdened with a crumb three times their size. He is there in the yeast, buried in the dough, wrapped in an old blanket, sitting in the sun to rise. *What is **not** God? Everything is infused with God.*

He is there in the smile of my wife as I open the door, coming home after work. He is there in the arms of my husband as he draws me close and we gently drift into sleep. He is there in the faces of the people I meet in my job, who stand behind me at the bank, whose prescriptions I fill. He is there as I dust and sweep and mop and straighten. He is there as I work in the garden, pulling weeds, packing soil around a plant, my hands clean with new dirt. He is there as I roller-blade around the lake, jog through the park, run, arms pumping and sweat pouring, along the side of the road. He is there, allowing my heart to listen to the pain and confusion and fear, behind the harsh words. *What is **not** God? Everything is infused with God.*

He is there is the nighttime sky, dressed in its velvet gown dusted with diamonds. He is there in the early dawn, as the sky, throwing off its crimson and gold cover, awakens. He is there in the song of the birds perched on the clothesline, singing songs to the sun. He is there as the baby mice frolic in the clear glass bowl in the shed, thinking they are unobserved. He is there in the steps of a toddler tottering on new-found feet, hands high above her head, maneuvering the tightrope of walking. He is there in the mind of an aging parent struggling with forgetfulness, tugging at our heartstrings. He is there as the years slide by and we blink our eyes and find that we are grandparents. *What is **not** God? Everything is infused with God.*

Everywhere I look, if I look with my heart and not just with my eyes, I can see God. Everything I hear, if I listen with my heart, and not just with my ears, I can hear God. Everything is infused with God; I have but to listen and see.

Today I am going to see God/Allah in everything.

The Mystic Ties of Parent and Child

Allah has given the mystic ties of parent and child. Sura. 90:30

There is a thread stronger than tinseled steel that binds a parent to his/her child. It is unexplainable; it is unbreakable; it endures forever– perhaps even beyond the grave. At the exact moment that you first cradle your new baby in your arms, there is a *mystic tie* that wraps around your heart and the heart of your child: a gift - a blessing from Allah.

I think that God knows exactly which child and which parents should be matched. He knows exactly who will love this little one as He loves him/her. He knows exactly whom to entrust with one of His precious little ones: gifts and blessings from Allah.

This love– this *mystic tie* –is hard to explain. We don't choose our parents or our children. They are somehow *written* into our lives by a Divine Scribe. We are linked by God to be parent and child. Into some of our lives are written daughters; into some of our lives are written sons; into some of our lives a mixture of daughters and sons- all precious, all gifts from Allah. Into most of our lives are written children who are biologically ours, into some of our lives are written children who are not biologically ours- yet in every important way *are* our sons and daughters. All are children of our hearts...dearly loved, as they are placed in our hearts by God. They are gifts and blessings from Allah.

I know the love of a parent for a child endures beyond the grave. My wife died when our children were seven and five but I *know* that she has continued to watch over them through the years; that she has been there for their high school graduations; that she has been there for their college commencements; that she was present when they got married; that she was there when her grandchildren were born.

I know the love of a parent for a child endures beyond the grave. I *know* that there are times when Allah lifts the veils between this life and the next to allow the love of a father for his son to pass through. I *know* that He has given a *mystic tie* that binds deceased father to living son. I *know* the father is there watching over his son; I know he was there when his son got married; I *know* he was there when his son became a father for the first time. I *know* the bond between this father and his son is unexplainable; it is unbreakable; it endures forever– even beyond the grave.

Allah has given the mystic ties of parent and child- unexplainable, unbreakable – ties that endure forever.

The Sum of Life

Nothing goes with you but the sum of what your life has been. <u>Essential Sufism,</u> p. 25

My father-in-law was a doctor and quite well-to-do --- at least people *said* he was. He had built five houses, one for each of his five daughters; yet he wouldn't allow my mother-in-law to hang curtains in all the rooms of their house – *too expensive.* Neighbors, even some of his relatives, would sigh and say: *He thinks he is going to take it with him, but all he is going to take is an old suit and new socks.* His sister-in-law, Auntie Nijmeh, had laid away in a bottom drawer of an old dresser the *things she wanted to be buried in:* a beautiful embroidered dress (laid away when she was slim), a beautiful embroidered head shawl and new underwear. She would occasionally take out the clothes and air them sighing: *This is all I am going to take with me.*

I ended up burying both. The only things that went with them were the clothes in which they were laid out, clean underwear and *new socks.* Nothing went with them *but the sum of what their lives had been.*

They may have imagined the deeds of their lives recorded in a ledger: the good deeds carefully listed on the plus side; the bad deeds subtracted from the sum; a column of addition and subtraction—credits and debits leading to an ultimate total. I think they believed that when they got to the *Pearly Gates* the ledger would be opened and read and their entrance depended on the *sum of what their lives had been.* (Granted, a rather simplistic way of looking at life, yet powerful.)

It isn't really about the material things we leave behind, but about the lives we have touched. It is *how* we are remembered: were we funny and loving, generous and thoughtful, or complaining and critical, unloving, tight-fisted and thoughtless?

We each are given a certain period of time– a certain number of days. What we do with those days is up to us. It is up to us how we treat those with whom we come in contact. It is up to us the words we choose to use when speaking to others– whether it is our spouse, or our children, or the faceless stranger on the other end of the phone. We choose to live our lives as we see fit. We *write* the stories of our lives. We take nothing with us but the sum of what our lives have been.

40

Borrowed Time

> *One dies when, by Allah's will, one's borrowed time ends. One's material being– which is called life– ending at an appointed hour loses all its character and qualities both good and bad, and nothing remains. That is what the Prophet of Allah (may peace and blessing be upon him) meant when he said, **Die before dying.*** Ibn' Arabi, Essential Sufism, p. 252

I can still hear my mother's voice warning me to do two things: *Never leave dishes in the sink, you don't know if you will die today or not; what would the neighbors think to find the sink full of dishes!* And the classic warning about *clean underwear and being run over by a truck.* Rather a sobering way of looking at life, but I am in my seventh decade and *still* leave the sink free of dishes when I go to work wearing clean underwear. You never know when that truck is going to come.

In a very simple way, she was expressing the philosophy of *borrowed time ending* and to *die before dying.* We need to be ready. It isn't really a pessimistic way of viewing life; it is merely recognizing that life is indeed *fragile* and death, most often, takes us unawares.

I have lived in the Middle East all my adult life. I have learned that there is certainly truth in the word, *inshallah* (God willing). *I'll see you after work, inshallah. We'll meet for dinner, inshallah. I am going to visit the kids in the States, inshallah.* There is this underlying belief that God governs whatever happens to us, and that we will do things if *God is willing.* It is acknowledging the constant presence of God and submission to His will.

The idea of *borrowed time* is meaningful. Some days we are tempted to think that we will live forever---we *know* that we will die, but often we *don't really believe it.* And, it is certainly a long way off, surely. But if we *knew* we only had so many months, or weeks, or days, or hours, how differently would we use this *borrowed* time? What are the things we would do if we *knew* we were dying? Tell those we love, daily, that we love them? Of course. Pick up the phone and call someone out of the blue? Perhaps. Be generous with our compliments and hugs? Maybe. Be sure the furniture is dusted and the plants deadheaded? Not so sure. We *would* do those things that had meaning for us and for those who are part of our lives. If our days were numbered (*and they are!*), we might live them differently. There is certain truth in the line: *die before dying.*

Each day when I go out the door, I glance into the central hall to be sure everything is in order– the prayer rug is laying across the back of the couch at a proper angle and the pillows are fluffed (anal retentive I know). I am sure there are no coffee cups in the sink, and I know I am wearing clean underwear in case I step in front of that truck. Every morning, for a fleeting moment, I think: *maybe today is the day my borrowed time ends.*

Inshallah we will use our borrowed time well.

He Sees You!

Worship God as if you see Him, and remember that even if you see Him not, He still sees you. Hadith: Words of the Prophet, <u>Essential Sufism,</u> p. 90

When my children were little I brainwashed them into thinking that I could *see everywhere, even when I wasn't in the room.* In the classes I taught, I warned the students at the beginning of the year that I *had eyes in the back of my head and I could see everything.* There is something in the concept of *being watched – being seen.* If we think we aren't being observed, we might be tempted to do things we wouldn't want to be caught doing! There is something about human nature that makes us want to *appear good.*

Sometimes it seems as though we don't *see* God, yet we are called upon to *worship Him.* The words of the Prophet (Peace and blessing be upon him) tell us to: *worship God as if you see Him.* The key words seem to be: *as if* – implying that perhaps we don't. We certainly see where God has been; we have but to look around us and see the beauty that surrounds us. We *see* His footprints and fingerprints along the paths that we walk. We *know* He is there. We *know* He is here. There are times when we can *feel* His presence.

It is important to know that even if we don't *see* Him, He still sees us. It probably goes a long way toward *keeping us good!* We wouldn't want our children, our colleagues, or neighbors, or best friends seeing *some* of the things we do, would we? Probably ninety percent of the time our lives are that proverbial *open book,* but that *other* ten percent?

It is soothing to my spirit to know that God can *see* my confusion, my frustration, my pain, the times when I am less than what He would have me be. It is soothing to my spirit to know that He *understands* and *forgives* and *loves* me just as I am. It is soothing to my spirit to realize that I really don't have to *explain* or *rationalize* my feelings, and thus my behavior. He knows me better than I know myself; even when I may not see Him, *He still sees me!* How wonderful that is!

I worship God. I am conscious of His presence. I am thankful that neither I, nor those I value, and care for and love, are ever alone.

I am going to try and live my life today as though God is looking over my shoulder for He is!

The Creator makes no Mistakes

He who knows three things is saved from three things: He who knows that the Creator made no mistakes at Creation is saved from petty fault finding. He who knows that He made no favoritism in allotting fortune is saved from jealousy. He who knows of what he is created is saved from pride. Ansari, Essential Sufism, p. 109

Petty fault-finding, jealousy, and pride: most of us are guilty of all three– at least sometimes. We look at someone and may say, or at least think; *well at least I am not like that!* It is easy to criticize someone's weight, or temperament, or intelligence, or the way he/she thinks, or the people he/she falls in love with.

It is easy to look at someone's beautiful home, fancy car, expensive cell phones and iPads; speculate about their outrageous salaries and the tuition spent to send their kids to prestigious schools and be jealous. We may think: *God has favored them above me.* I'm looking in garbage bins for cast offs and recyclables; I don't have a flat screen TV or a fancy car; I still have a rotary phone, and eating out may be a trip to *McDonald's* or *Pizza Hut*. And then I look at the news and see the conditions in Somalia, starving children with glockenspiel rib cages and balloon stomachs; I look at the news and see people lounging in their deck chairs beside the swimming pool in one place, and a little girl waiting to fill her plastic container with water in another. I certainly don't understand how some people seem to have so much and others seem to have so little. I suppose it all *balances out in the long run,* yet...

The Quran is very graphic and realistic in stating that man is the outcome of a *liquid despised* and a *clot.* The Bible states that *man is molded from dust and clay* and both state that to *dust we return.* I suppose, looked at in that light, we are *saved from pride.*

I don't *want* to be petty and find fault; I don't *want* to be jealous and envy anyone; I don't *want* to be vain and prideful, but I am guilty of all. I *do believe* that God/Allah makes no mistakes and that He has created us just as He has seen fit and I would hope that this knowledge makes me more tolerant of everyone; women who choose to cover their faces, and folks who choose to wedge wooden plates into their lower lips and wear brass rings to stretch their necks. I would pray that this would make me more accepting of different religions that allow plural marriage or the growing of side curls. I would wish that this knowledge would make me more understanding of peoples' sexual orientation and what really constitutes a family. I really am not in a position to find fault with anyone based on how God fashioned them.

I can remember my father saying about someone who was boastful and full of pride: *He must think his poop don't stink.* I don't think anyone has a reason to be boastful and prideful. One can take pride in one's work – but that is different than boasting and being vain.

I would pray today that I would be free of petty fault-finding, free of jealousy and harmful pride.

An Instrument for another's Growth

Sufis say that this world can be heaven– when we love and bless one another, serve one another and become the instruments for one's inner growth and salvation. <u>Essential Sufism,</u> p. 73

My youngest is a born gardener. He loves getting his hands dirty with good clean dirt; he loves laying out the plots and deciding what to plant; he loves the way things, when watered and nurtured, grow – he is landscaping his home into a wee bit of Eden – a patch of heaven. His home is a place soothing to the spirit, fragrant with the perfume of flowers, yet practical with ripe tomatoes and lush berries kissed by the sun. He has created his own bit of heaven.

It is in our power to create our own bits of heaven- not just with the physical surroundings, though this certainly helps, but with how we deal with each other. We all know people who make us *feel good,* people who seem to energize us and give us that proverbial *shot in the arm.* Years ago, whenever I would feel a little down, I would go to see Hasna. Hasna had eight children, couldn't read or write, and was a widow. She had this amazing spirit! To be in her presence seemed to put everything in perspective. There was a warmth about her that was soothing to my spirit. Whenever I would visit her, I felt that I had – for a brief moment--had a glimpse of heaven. I always felt that she had contributed to my inner growth. She had this gift of caring. Her life was a blessing to her children and to those around her.

Whenever I walk from home to school or from home to the store or just go for my daily walks, I ask Allah to bless those I pass. I am a people watcher. I look at people and try to imagine what their lives are like. I see a young mother carrying a baby, a toddler pulling at her skirts, and obviously pregnant – and in passing I say in my mind: *May Allah bless you and give you strength.* I pass a man on the street with a purple stain on his otherwise handsome face, and in my mind say: *May Allah bless you today.* There is a young man who sells newspapers out of a baby carriage. He is severely handicapped. Every day he is sitting in the same spot. Every day I smile and ask him how he is and tell him: *May God be with you.* Coming home from school the other day, in front of me was a neighbor woman. She is in her seventies; quite heavy; sweating from the heat and the walk from the market. She was carrying two shopping bags and struggling up the hill toward home. I stopped and took her bags from her and we chatted as we walked toward home. It is the little acts of blessing and service that can help create a bit of heaven here. It is small, yet meaningful.

Every day when I email the children I tell them how much they are loved; I tell them to *feel the love that surrounds them.* Every time I talk to the children on the phone, or to my siblings, I tell them: *love ya. This world can be heaven – when we love and bless one another.*

We also have the power to make this world a hell for others when we chew someone out, when we are critical and complain, when we are always negative, when we are unsmiling and rude. We have the power to make this world a bit of heaven, or a glimpse of hell. It is up to us.

48

Today, I am going to bless and love others; I am going to serve others; I am hopefully going to be the instrument for another's growth.

Opening the Eyes of the Heart

When the eyes of the heart open, we can see the inner realities hidden behind the outer forms of this world. When the ears of the heart open, we can hear what is hidden behind words: we can hear truth. <u>Essential Sufism,</u> p. 101

Every Monday evening, without fail, the phone rings. It is always the same person; it is always the same conversation. The caller is a former colleague, a woman I worked with in 1965 when I was still a student in college. She and her sister are now, quite reluctantly, in a nursing home. Every Monday she makes the trip back to her former home, shops, and spends the night. Every Tuesday I go across town, and carry her two shopping bags to the bus back to the nursing home. It is the same routine every Tuesday.

Every Tuesday I argue with her that the trip is too long, the summer is too hot, and she needs to take care. (She has been warned by the doctor that she should not make the trip.) She is stubborn; she is obstinate; she is deaf to reason. When the eyes and ears of my heart are open I can see the truth: she is lonely; she doesn't want to be in the nursing home; she sees her life as over and looks back with regret. She makes *excuses* to make these weekly trips: *the nuns are starving us; I need to come to buy food or we will perish; I need to buy aspirin; I need to dust the furniture.* I have tried to convince her to come once a month, or every two weeks, to combine her errands. She *needs* to come every week – it is her lifejacket as she treads water drowning in the sea of old age, and dependence and loneliness. She needs to call every Monday evening. She needs to hear that I will come on Tuesday afternoon, as I always do, and walk her to the bus.

We need to learn to *see* with our hearts behind the façade that masks the inner reality. We need to become attuned to listening with the *ears* of our hearts to the meaning behind the words spoken. We have been schooled to act a certain way, to say certain words, to veil our realities. We don't want to be exposed, for to be exposed makes us vulnerable. If we are vulnerable, we are presumed weak; if we are weak we will be walked on and hurt. It is almost automatic to respond to: *How are you?* With: *Fine, couldn't be better* when the reality is far from fine, and when often the person asking is not really interested in how we are. I like the Arabic response to the question: *illhumdillah* (praise God) or *nush'kur Allah* (we thank God). It recognizes no matter the situation or condition, God is aware and we are not alone and we are thankful – even though at times it is somewhat said with a sigh and a bit of resignation.

I think in many ways Allah opens our hearts to see and hear the truth and to respond; with a hug, with a listening ear that doesn't criticize or blame, with understanding and tolerance, with sympathy and acceptance, with reassurance that *this too will pass,* and perhaps, with the most important gift of all –*time;* time to see, time to listen, time that lets the other person know he or she is not alone.

Today, I pray that my heart will be open to see the inner reality, and to hear the truth behind the words.

The Angel of Death

When the angel of death came to take Abraham's soul, Abraham said. "Have you ever seen a friend take his friend's soul?" God answered him, "Have you ever seen a friend unwilling to meet or go with his friend?" Al-Ghazzali, Essential Sufism, p.252

Abraham is a religious forefather in Judaism, Christianity and Islam. Each share the belief in an Angel of Death coming to take the soul of a person when *it is written* that his/her borrowed time is over. In the imagined conversation between God and Abraham, there is the concept of *friendship* – intimacy. Abraham is questioning, almost scolding, *I thought we were friends, yet you've sent the Angel of Death to take my soul!* Allah responds also with a question, also slightly scolding: *Friends want to go with each other!* I like the hint of intimacy between God and Abraham – the easiness that exists between friends. I like the underlying belief that death is *a meeting of friends.*

Death comes to us all. For some it comes when it seems the person has barely had a touch of living; it seems that their candle is barely lit when the flame is blown out. For some it comes in their prime– in the vigor and strength of their young adulthood when they still seem to have so much to do: a family to raise, a spouse and children to love. For some it comes when the candle has melted away and the flame flickers and dances in a pool of melted wax. It seems that the time is right. Death comes for us all.

My wife was diagnosed with cancer when the children were quite small. A lump on her breast was misdiagnosed as a milk nodule. When the reality was discovered, it was too late and we prepared for her passage into the next phase of living. We talked a lot about death and dying and about a future apart. We used to joke when the children were little and we were frustrated about something they had done: *I'm going before you!* Now it was a truth, she was going before me and leaving me with young children.

The last month of her dying, daily she would ask, *What am I doing wrong? Why am I lingering?* I would kneel before her in the rocking chair and rest my head in her lap and assure her she was doing nothing wrong, that death would come for her and what *an adventure it would be.*

The night before she died she was in a half-dream state. It seemed as though she was having a conversation with relatives who had died. In the snatches of conversation, she would smile and say: *I am so glad you are waiting for me —I won't be long — I'm coming.* The afternoon she died she was quite restless (perhaps anxious to be off on her journey.) I gave the prescribed shot of morphine for the pain. She motioned me to lower my head so she could whisper in my ear. She could barely speak, but the words were clear: *I'm going before you.* I lay down beside her on the bed and drew her into my arms; she gave a contented sigh and slipped into heaven. She was off on yet another adventure— an adventure in the company of friends.

Death for us, for those we love, is a *welcomed meeting of friends.*

A thousand-stringed Instrument

The heart is a thousand-string instrument that can only be tuned with love. From "The Thousand-Stringed Instrument" The Gift: Poems by Hafiz, p.228

We always had a piano at home. At first it was an old, heavy upright that someone gave my mother for only $5. For another $5 she had it tuned, and I can still hear her playing *I'm the Last of the Red-hot Mamas,* and singing hymns. It was her comfort through the years of poverty, and childrearing and wearing *tent-size* dresses. She later, when I was about eight, bought a brand new piano on installments. It now sits in my daughter's home, the keys rather stiff, slightly out of tune, but the strings can still vibrate with *My Funny Valentine* and *It's Only a Shanty in Old Shanty Town.*

One watches the string instruments being tuned before the orchestra performs. The violinist holds the strings close to the ear – listening – as the key is turned to tighten or loosen the tension. *The heart is a thousand-string instrument that can only be tuned with love.* Imagine tuning a *thousand strings!* Listening...turning the key or the small pliers first this way, then back, then this way again, always listening for when it seems in tune.

The Sufi poet, Hafiz, lived in Persia in the fourteenth century. He writes in his poem, *The Thousand-Stringed Instrument,* that "Our sadness and fear come from being out of tune with love. When we are *out of tune* with God we become sad and afraid --- sad over events in our lives, afraid of what the present is and what the future may be – unhappy, depressed, stressed-out, unaware that God/Allah *is* in the moment – *is* in the now – and *will be there* in the future. Our hearts, with the thousands of thoughts and feelings --- images, impressions, hurts, pains – that *thousand-string instrument* can *only be tuned with love.*

You swing your toddler up into your arms and he/she nestles his/her head on your shoulder, the curls brushing your cheek as a small arm encircles your neck –a string of your heart is tuned with love. You kiss your spouse; you hug a friend; you clasp someone's hand in a firm, strong handshake – a string of your heart is tuned with love. You smile at the customer who waits to be served; you joke with the waitress who takes your order, you say hello to the stranger filling his tank as you fill yours – a string of your heart is tuned with love.

Allah has ninety-nine names in Islam. One of them perhaps should be *Musician.* It is He who gives the birds the songs they sing to the dawn, the music the crickets play as they rub the violin strings of their legs, the bass notes of the bullfrogs, and the anthems of the nightingale. It is He who has created our hearts as a *thousand-string instrument* capable of producing heavenly music – reminiscent of angel songs. It is up to us to keep our instrument in tune so we can reproduce the heavenly music He has placed in our hearts.

The heart is a thousand-string instrument that can only be tuned with love.

Blind Spots

Even the most clear-sighted have blind spots. <u>Essential Sufism</u>, p. 57

At times, in my own mind, I think that I am probably the *most clear-sighted* individual I know. I can *look* at a situation through my bifocals – even when they aren't sitting on my nose correctly—and *instinctively know* what I should do, and certainly what *someone else* should do. Blind spots? Certainly not! (Sure, that's as true as *birds can swim and dogs can fly.)*

Even the most clear-sighted amongst us have blind spots. All of us have times when we don't really see the situation as it is. We look right at it, but we don't *see* what is in front of us. I am biased toward my children. I may see what they do and rationalize their actions. I may see what their spouses sometimes do and think: *Well, why in the world are they doing that!* I know I am sometimes biased when it comes to my grandchildren; I can see what they do and think: *Well, they are just kids,* while I may look at other children and think: *Where are their parents? That little one needs an old fashioned warm bottom.* Most of the time I really am fairly clear-sighted, but I do have my *blind spots.*

We obviously see the world through glasses that have been tinted by our childhood experiences and our adult situations; glasses that have been colored by how we were raised, our own temperament, and our present circumstances. We aren't naïve; we don't see the world through those proverbial *rose-colored* glasses. However, we do most likely view the world through lenses that have been scratched, or smudged, or tinted.

We are prejudiced when we think that our religious beliefs are the only *right ones.* We are insular when we think that our society, in spite of its flaws, is the only *right one.* We are short-sighted when we think that the way we do something is the only *right way. Even the most clear-sighted have blind spots.*

I was in DC, among the thousands, when Martin Luther King gave his famous *I have a dream* speech. Thousands were inspired by his words, yet equally well-meaning people thought he was an upstart Negro. I was an anti-Vietnam protestor; I can still hear in my mind's ear the words of one of my veteran brothers: *If I was on the opposite side of the picket line, I would kill you.* My daughter and her husband were in a restaurant. There at the bar sat a man wearing a t-shirt with the words: *Nuke Arabs.* She is an attractive, soft-spoken woman. She went up to him and told him she *just wanted to know what prejudice looked like.* He was a teacher! I am sure he thought he was seeing a situation clearly. He was oblivious to his blind spot.

Today, I would wish to be aware of my *blind spots* and pray that I would be truly *clear-sighted.*

Life: A Stage-by-Stage Journey

Man's life never rests here below, but travels ever onward stage by stage. Sura 84:19

My oldest son was relating the exploits of his four year old. The little one- bright, engaging, challenging- knows which buttons to push to get a reaction from his parents. It seems that he is always *testing* to see just where the perimeters are and how much he can get away with. I asked my son who his son reminded him of. He paused, and I could hear the laughter in his voice, '*Me, when I was four.*' *Life never rests here below, but travels ever onward stage by stage.*

Shakespeare's memorable line: *All the world's a stage, and all men and women merely players...and one man in his time plays many parts,* is certainly true. We play the role of child, of adolescent, of son or daughter, of a newly married adult, of a parent, of a grandparent. Life *travels ever onward stage by stage.* We begin life as an infant dependent upon others for survival. We sometimes end life once again childlike– dependent upon others for survival. We spend the middle years, hopefully, strong and active and independent. Others may depend on us.

Sometimes we anxiously embrace the next stage: being old enough to drive; old enough to earn our own money; old enough to make our own decisions. Sometimes we cling to the past, dragging our feet into the next stage: we color our hair; have false teeth and hair implants, perhaps liposuction – we want to *look young.* We feel complimented when someone says, *My you don't look your age!* (I tutored a youngster one year. He asked me how old I was. I asked him how old he thought I was. He replied: *Ninety.* Shocked, I asked him: *Do I look ninety?* I am still chuckling about his reply: *No, you look a hundred. I didn't want to hurt your feelings.* Life never rests here below, but travels ever onward stage by stage.

It can be wonderful to grow old– if we have the right attitude. It is a time when one is finally free to be one's self; hopefully free of wanting to *appear* differently than we really are. We can get away with a lot of things because we are *old.* Age can be a grand excuse for doing the eccentric, for *being eccentric.* For years I was a closet knitter. Now, I knit in front of anyone. One of my students saw me knitting and asked: *Sir, you knit?!* I replied of course. *It is a manly activity. The first knitters were Arab shepherds watching their sheep; then sailors on long voyages, then British craftsmen before the invention of knitting machines. Knitting was a male occupation before it became a female pastime.*

Each passing stage takes us closer to reunion with God/Allah. Each stage is precious and should be enjoyed. We should learn to embrace each new stage with joy. God willing, we will grow old gracefully- perhaps old in body but youthful in mind and spirit. *Life never rests here below, but travels ever onward stage by stage.* I pray that I embrace each stage with joy.

Fasting and Self-Restraint

O you who believe, fasting is prescribed to you as it was prescribed to those before you, so that you may learn self-restraint. Sura 2:183

It is like Christmas in August. Multicolored lights garland the street posts and stretch electric webs across the streets. Helium balloons in the shapes of donkeys and monkeys and whales are battered by the breeze and float and fly above the heads of shoppers. The streets are crowded with shoppers and gypsy-like sellers who spread their wares along the sidewalk. One can find *anything* from food processors, to sandals festooned with sequins, to bouquets of artificial flowers wrapped in cellophane, to American primitive toilet tissue holders and a pink box holding a blonde Barbie in her summer frock. Tomorrow or perhaps the day after marks the end of Ramadan- the month of fasting.

Fasting is one of the Five Pillars of Islam. The devout are expected, if they are able, to fast the entire month between dawn and dusk. No food, no water, no smoking, no sex, not even bad thoughts. One learns *self-restraint* – how to rule the natural demands of the body. One learns compassion– to feel with those less fortunate. One learns generosity – to share with those who are in need. One learns to make a real effort to be kind and thoughtful and to refrain from complaining and criticizing. One reads through the Quran gleaning new wisdom from the familiar words. One conscientiously prays five times a day. For me, it has always been a month of reflection and meditation, a time of soul-searching and, hopefully, self-improvement.

The month of Ramadan is often a time of joyous gathering of family and friends to break the fast and share *iftar*. Every evening at sunset family and friends share food and fellowship. It is a month of inviting and being invited. Even times I am alone, I find preparing my tray of food and drink and sitting in front of the television as a time of reflection and contemplation, a time of thankfulness for all the blessings that God/Allah has given.

O you who believe, fasting is prescribed to you as it was prescribed to those before you, so that you may learn self-restraint.

I have found the month of Ramadan to be a month of good self-discipline. There is no one to *see* if I take a sip of water during the day; there is no one to *see* if I get up just before dawn to have something to eat, something to drink; there is no one to *see* what I am thinking. Allah sees, and I see.

It is good to learn compassion; it is good to be kind and generous and to think of others; it is good to learn to control our cravings (even if it just be for caffeine and nicotine); it is good to learn self-restraint. Ramadan is a blessed month for those who believe.

Loving Care is Sure

He was content and consoled in the thought that Allah has bestowed His loving care on him in the past, and so the future was sure. Did He not find thee an orphan and give thee shelter and care? Sura 93:6

God/Allah has always taken care of us. Even in the darkest nights, He is there. Even when we feel most alone, He is there. Even when we doubt His presence, He is there.

I can look back at the events of my life, and the lives of my children, and see where Allah has always bestowed His loving care on me and on them. Even those times when I felt that His care and love were not evident, they were! I was a widower at a young age; left with young children to parent. There were times when I was *sure* that I wouldn't be able to cope; times when I reached the end of that proverbial *rope* and didn't even seem to have the strength, or the will, to tie a knot and hold on. It was just at those times that Allah seemed to reach out and touch the events in such a way that I felt consoled, cared for, loved. I can remember consciously saying the words in my mind: *Thank you God.*

I didn't know how we were going to manage financially; how I would save money for college educations on a one-parent income; how I would juggle being *mom* as well as dad; how I would manage being an *at-home* parent and an *at-work* parent. I hadn't really counted on God's/Allah's loving care. I was surprised to receive a call a month after my wife died, just before we were to return abroad, from someone in the Social Security office. She had read the obituary and wondered why I hadn't applied for survivor benefits for my children. I hadn't even known that was possible, since it was my wife who had died. I did apply, and the children received a small amount from their mother's social security. I religiously saved it for them and when it came time to go to college, there was the money! Allah provided. When I chose to return to work abroad in the same school where my children were students, it worked out perfectly. Their vacations were my vacations. They went with me to work, and came home with me after work. They never had to have a sitter; they never came home to an empty house. I was the at-home mom and the at-work dad. Allah's loving care was present. Recently, my oldest child, now in her thirties, commented that she had had a *wonderful childhood.* I was startled by her comment. She had lost her mother when she was seven; we had lived under military occupation; there were curfews, and uprisings– and still she could look back and make that comment. Allah's loving care had always been present.

As I look at my adult children and observe the struggles they face, I am *consoled in the thought that Allah has bestowed His loving care in the past, and so* their *future was sure.* I am positive that Allah has written wonderful things into their lives. He has written into my life *another child* --- a child who tragically lost his biological father when he was only twelve – Allah knew I needed another child to love, and perhaps another child who needed a substitute dad. That child is now married and a father himself. I thank Allah every day for each of my children, biological and not. Each day I am sure that Allah is always present, always loving, always caring. He has been present in the past, He is present in the now, and thus the future, no matter what happens, *is sure.*

Gifts from God

Sorrow and suffering may, if we take them rightly, turn out to be the best gifts of Allah to us. Sura 6:42

"No pain, no gain" is often the advice given by coaches, personal trainers, and weight managers. If we want change: a six-pack, toned muscles, and the only *spare tire* to be the one in the trunk of the car, we need to sweat, and pump, and feel the pain to get the gain. There has to be a bit of physical suffering.

I was visiting an old friend yesterday- a woman I have known since she was just a girl of fifteen. She is now fifty-one and the mother of eight. We were talking about the wrinkles that come in all relationships, especially in marriage. When she was first married she had three small children; she was swamped with babies and housework. At the time she thought her husband was insensitive and demanding. One day she packed her bags, dressed the kids and was opening the door to leave–key in hand. By chance, her mother stopped in. She saw the bags; she saw the grandchildren bundled up to leave; she saw the key in her daughter's hand. She heard her daughter say: *I can't take it anymore. I have suffered enough.* Her mother looked at her, took the key out of her hand, put it down the front of her dress and sat in a chair by the door. She told her daughter to make a cup of tea and that no one was going anywhere. She sat by the door until her daughter made up her mind to stay.

My friend said: *It was the best thing my mother could have done. Yes, I suffered at first. There were times when I wanted to cry most of the time. But I am so glad I stayed-we have been married for over twenty-five years. The sorrow and the suffering have made me a better person – in some ways it was a gift from Allah.*

One of the biggest regrets I have is beating my son when he was nine years old. It is always there in the back of my mind – my secret *scarlet letter.* We were living under occupation and there were often armed soldiers in jeeps patrolling the streets. One afternoon I glanced out of the dining room window and saw my nine year old throw stones at a jeep, and then duck behind a tree. The stone didn't reach the jeep. When he came in I asked him if he had been throwing stones. He answered, *No, Baba, I wasn't.* I beat him with my fists. I can still hear myself saying to him: *If anyone is going to kill you, it is going to be me.* He was crying. His sister was crying. I was crying. I hugged him and apologized and told him it would never happen again. And it never did. I still bear the scar of what I had done. It certainly wasn't a gift from Allah – but it did teach me a valuable lesson.

Years later when he was in college, I was questioning something he said to me. I asked him if he was lying to me. He replied: *The only time I every lied to you was that time when I was nine.* I had never forgotten, nor had he.

My grandmother used to say, and my mother repeat, *Sometimes our biggest disappointments are blessings in disguise.* We sometimes have to *search* for the blessing in a situation. When we fail, we learn. Hopefully, we try and try again until we succeed. We may learn endurance and strength through failure. When we put effort into making a marriage work rather than walking out the door we hope to become stronger and better able to face whatever obstacles arise, together; when we meet the struggles of childrearing- dealing with spilled milk and poop behind the couch, tantrums, and children pushing all the wrong buttons at all the wrong times and still hug them at night and kiss them as we put them to bed, we are teaching them that the world, in spite of everything, is a safe place because at the end of the day there is someone to hug us and kiss us good-night as we are tucked into bed.

Sometimes sorrow and suffering- when they strengthen us and help us grow and become better peoples- can be a *gift from Allah.*

Power over All Things

Allah has power over all things. Sura 32:17

I have a need to *believe* that God *has power over all things* this morning. There are mornings when I awaken from a restless night and feel that nothing is as it should be. I am discontent with myself, disgruntled with people and situations, discouraged – for a moment feeling that *nothing will ever be right* –right as I perceive it and wish it to be. There are mornings when, like Christian in *Pilgrim's Progress,* I am sliding down into the *Slough of Despair.* The sides are slippery and there is no way that I will be able to crawl out. I need to believe that *Allah has power over all things.*

I have a need to *believe* this morning that everything is going to be ultimately all right for my children, for their spouses, for their children. That the wrinkles that are in their lives will be ironed out, and their lives will be as they should be, as I daily pray they will be. I want them to be happy and healthy, prosperous and content. There are times when I want to *bargain* with God– thinking if I say, or do, or promise the right thing, the children will be happy and healthy and prosperous and content. I need to believe that *Allah has power over all things.*

I have a need to *believe* this morning that Allah has a magic wand, and that with a wave and the proper incantation, my children's lives will be wrinkle-free, stress-free, frustration-free, clutter-free; their lives will be perfect as only Allah can make them! I need to believe that *Allah has power over all things.*

I look at some situations and can't seem to envision the solution. I look at some lives and can't see how change is possible; there is too much baggage, too much past, too many cobwebs in the mind unreachable by the sweep of my broom. I need to believe that *Allah has power over all things.*

Thankfully, there are most mornings when I awaken and am aware of Allah's power to transform, to wave His wand and magically, so it seems, make the impossible possible, the unchangeable changed, the hopeless hopeful. I know He has *power over all things.* I know that nothing is *carved in stone*...nothing is unalterable...I know that people change, situations change, that one can crawl out of that *Slough of Despair* and throw off depression, discouragement, discontentedness, disgruntled-ness, despair. I know that *Allah has power over all things.*

I have a need to believe that this morning. And I do.

All will come Right, in Good Time

All will come right in good time; so persevere with patient firmness of purpose. Justice that seems to tarry comes really on swiftest foot but sure. The Glorious Quran, p. 1365.

My mother, newly married, just eighteen wanted to impress my father by baking a pie. She mixed up the dough, tried to roll it out, couldn't get it to roll. She covered the enamel dishpan with a clean dishtowel and put the basin behind the barn. She tried again: mixed the dough; tried to roll it. It still wouldn't roll, so she added it to the dough in the enamel dishpan behind the garage. This went on several times. When Dad got home from work, Mother was sitting in a rocking chair on the porch crying. She told Dad the story of the pie dough. He went behind the barn and there was the enamel dishpan overflowing with dough. He brought it in, added some water, a little bit of flour, and gently worked it with his rough, carpenter's hands. Patiently he worked the dough. Eventually mother rolled out enough for six pies. Patiently they persevered. It all came right in good time. This is a simple story. Mother went on to win prizes for her pies at country fairs; her daughter and one of her sons became excellent pie bakers. Perseverance and patient firmness of purpose became the motto. I can still hear my mother saying: *Keep trying, you'll get it. Rome wasn't built in a day. It will all be right in God's good time.*

Things have a way of working out- of coming right - all in good time. Often we get impatient. We want immediate solutions to our problems; instant results; prompt feedback. We want the house built, the college degree, the high-paying executive job, the A on the test, to play the piano without practicing and to be the star athlete without the grueling workouts; perfect, well-mannered children without the effort of childrearing. The key to any achievement is to *patiently persevere with firmness of purpose.* We need to keep telling ourselves that *we can do it;* we have to keep struggling, persevering patiently – not giving up. We have to believe that *all will come right in good time.*

I keep telling my children this; I keep telling them that everything will come right in Allah's good time that they need to keep working at it, that they need to be patient, that they need to be firm in their purpose, not just waiting for it to happen, but working toward the goals they have set for themselves.

At times we think that we live in an unjust world. There is tyranny; there is an imbalance of wealth and power; there are military occupations; there is discrimination; there are people who are not treated as they should be as children of God. Sometimes it seems as though the cheats and the liars are the ones who win. But ultimately, so I believe, there *is justice* and people will reap the results of the seeds they have sown. We are responsible for our actions, and sometimes *justice that seems to tarry comes really on swiftest foot:* the tyrant is overthrown, military occupations end, discrimination fades, the cheaters and liars are caught in their lies. Things do have a way of working out - all in God's good time. We must persevere, be firm of purpose and be patient.

All that is in Men's Hearts

In the end to your Lord is your return when He will tell you
the truth of all that you did in this life. For He knows well all
that is in men's hearts. Sura 39:7

We all return to Allah in the end. The earthly journey begins at
birth, then there are the years of probation where we grow and
strive and struggle in our quest to survive and live, and ends with
our physical death and the spiritual journey back to God. In those
intervening years, we hopefully learn to be kind and generous,
thoughtful and sensitive, tolerant and loving.

Of course, the years are marked with physical living: the acquiring
of material things that make our lives easier and become symbolic
of our work and success; the earning of diplomas and degrees that
hopefully give us financial security and independence; the learning
of skills that develop our talents and marketability; developing a
spiritual life that transforms us from within, that acknowledges the
Divine, that recognizes that there is a Power beyond ourselves; the
practicing of a prayer-life consciously linking us to the Divine. In
those years of earthly probation we are given the opportunity to *be*
the hands and arms and legs and words of Allah's ambassadors. He
can use us to show His kindness, His mercy, His compassion, His
forgiveness, His tolerance, His thoughtfulness, His generosity for all.

He will tell you the truth of all you did in this life. God/Allah knows
what is in our hearts. He knows the motivation behind the acts. He
knows the sincerity, or lack thereof, behind the words. He *sees*

inside our hearts; we can't hide the truth of all that we do. We often rationalize to ourselves the reasons for our actions: *It was the way I was raised; My mother never had time for me; My father never accepted me; I was abused as a child; I was never understood; I never had his breaks, or her beauty, or their money; It really isn't my fault that I am the way I am, that I think the way I think, that I do the things I do.* How often do we say: *Well, that wasn't what I meant* (when it probably was what we meant), or, *I have to be honest, I don't want to be critical or hurt you, but...* (when in reality we *do* want to be critical, to tell them off, to let them know how it is; we *do* want to hurt them *just a little* – after all, they hurt us) or, my favorite: *this hurts me more than it hurts you.* Allah will tell us the truth of all we did in this life, for He knows well all that is in our hearts.

He knows when we are in pain, when we are frustrated and confused, when we are angry and wanting to lash out; He is compassionate, and merciful, and forgiving, for He knows well all that is in our hearts, and He will tell us the truth of all that we do and did in this life.

In the end to your Lord is your return when He will tell you the truth of all that you did in this life. For He knows well all that is in men's hearts. I would pray today that I would know the truth behind all I do. I would pray today that I could see into my own heart and see the truth that is there. I would pray today that I would be conscious that in the end my journey is a return to Allah; I would pray, today, that I would be aware of the truth that He is with me all through the journey, not just at the beginning, and not just at the end.

The Tongue and the Truth It Speaks

They say with their tongue what is not in their heart. Sura
48:11

We are taught to be *nice* and to tell *white lies. How do you like my outfit?* Beautiful. *How do you like my cake?* Delicious. *Hope you aren't busy?* No, I'm glad you called. *Did I wake you?* No, I've been up for hours. (As we stifle a yawn and rub sleep from our eyes.) We have been taught to be polite, to compliment, to not say exactly what is on the tip of our tongues and what is really in our hearts.

For minor things it probably doesn't really matter; perhaps sometimes it would be almost better to tell a white lie. My mother got quite heavy after the birth of her first child. She went from 110 pounds to 220 pounds and never lost the weight. One time she was buying a housedress. The clerk asked her what size; my father was standing there and, thinking it a joke said, *Tent size.* In almost sixty years of marriage, she never forgot those words. I've never forgotten the story and the lesson it taught. Maybe sometimes it is better to say nothing.

We are taught to *watch what we say* if we care about a relationship– unless saying what is in our hearts could ultimately *help* clarify a situation. We are taught *not to say what is in our hearts* for fear we will be misunderstood, or misinterpreted, or judged- at least until we are old and don't care anymore what people may think.

I have thankfully, almost joyfully, reached the age where I can almost *get away with murder.* I can say what I think and it is often chalked up to: *well, he's old.* My tongue and heart are often in harmony, because I am old. It can be very freeing as people know that I am going to be honest (although I still try to be kind with the words my tongue speaks.)

Perhaps if we always, in kindness, and with sensitivity, honestly revealed what is in our hearts, relationships would be better; parents and children would understand each other better, friends would be better friends, neighbors would be better neighbors, and people would know they could trust one another. Rather than carrying resentment around to fester, we could explain kindly and with sensitivity, how we are seeing a situation, and how we are *hearing* the words that are being said– so there could be clarification and perhaps acknowledgement, *that wasn't what I meant, I am sorry that that was what you heard.*

When I was a child, growing up where there were communities of Pennsylvania Dutch (Amish) who lived in the area. We used to use the phrase: *Talk to him like a Dutch uncle.* The Amish were known for always being honest and speaking the simple truth. To talk to someone like a *Dutch uncle* meant to be perfectly honest and say what was in your heart. We perhaps should talk to each other like *Dutch Uncles*- while always remembering to be *kind and sensitive,* the words we speak should reflect *what is in our hearts.*

Hidden Delights

No person knows what delights of the eye are kept hidden in reserve for him as a reward for their good deeds. Sura 32:17

I keep telling my children that *Allah has written amazing things into their lives.* I know it is true. They are going to be startled by the wonderful blessings which will be theirs. I want them to be aware of all the blessings that envelope them: the coolness of a rain after a particularly hot day; the scent of a rose as its bud unfolds, the beauty of a sunset as though God has been splashing the sky with vibrant swathes from his pallet, the smell of a baby fresh from its bath, the feel of a little fist curled around your finger. I want them to be aware of the small, everyday things that bless their lives.

I keep telling my children that they don't really know *what delights are kept hidden in reserve for* them --- simply because they are good --- simply because they are loved --- simply because they are precious in the sight of God. We want the best for our children. If we want the best for them, how much more does Allah want the best for them?

I look for ways to make my children happy. I look for ways to let them know that they are thought of; that they are valued; that they are cared for, that they are loved. I look for things that might delight their eyes and touch their hearts. If I do this, how much more will Allah hold in reserve *delights of the eye for them!*

I am at peace knowing that God/Allah loves my children; knowing that He is watching out for them, guiding them, holding them in His light; knowing that He will always care for them, that He will always bless their lives. I am at peace, knowing that He has written amazing things into their lives – more than they could hope for or envision. I am at peace, knowing that he has hidden in reserve for them delights of the eye as a reward for their good deeds.

Today I will be at peace. Allah loves my children. Allah guides my children. Allah values my children. Allah has written into their lives amazing, wonderful, startling things. They will be surprised by what He has hidden in reserve for them.

The Birds and their Prayers

The birds of the air, with wings outspread, know their own mode of prayer and praise. Sura 24:41

In some places in the world, thanks to dryers and suburban restrictions, clotheslines are a thing of the past, like Granny's calico apron and curtain stretchers. Thankfully, I still have lines strung, and can still hang the wash and have it buffeted by the breeze and kissed by the sun. I even have lines threaded across the veranda for those days when it is rainy and the clothes may need a bit of roof over them.

The lines on the veranda are not often used. They are there, among plants and vines that hang and creep among the bars. They are there above the old, wooden bench from the Quaker Meeting House, above the antique rocker with its backward rockers, above the old, wicker chair and metal yard stool from a hotel's glory days. The lines on the veranda are not often used. Not often used to hang the *wash* that is. They are used every morning as the choir loft for birds. Just as dawn is beginning to break over the horizon, the birds begin to take their places along the clothesline. They clear their throats, chat to one another, and then – almost as though there is a choir master, they begin their songs of prayer and praise. *The birds of the air, with wings outspread, know their own mode of prayer and praise.*

Every morning, just as the day is throwing off its colorful covers, I sit at my desk and write emails to my children. It is a morning ritual.

Every morning, just as the day is awakening from its slumber, I sit at my desk and listen to the birds sing their songs of prayer and praise.

I think that all of God's creatures *know their own mode of prayer and praise.* Every morning I pause and think about the prayers the birds are praying. How thankful they must be, for though they neither *toil nor spin,* Allah takes care of them.

Some evenings, as the wind whispers through the branches of the trees outside my window, I can almost hear their prayers. Some evenings as the rain gently falls against the tiles of the roof, I can almost hear its praise. I think all of nature has its own mode of prayer and praise. Everything is God, and God is in everything.

Today I will tune my ear to hear the birds as they sing their praises to God and pray. I will clear my eyes to see the flowers as they nod and bend their heads in prayer. I will hear the prayers that are whispered in the branches of the tree. *The birds of the air, with wings outspread, know their own mode of prayer and praise.* So do I.

No cause for Secrecy

The righteous have no cause for secrecy, except in doing good. Sura 4:108

If we are honest, if we are straight-forward, if we are righteous, we *have no cause for secrecy.* Our life should be that proverbial *open book;* it should be transparent, there should be no need for secrecy; no reason to hide who we are, and what we have done. Think how freeing it could be to have no secrets– to have nothing to hide- nothing which we are reluctant to have others know- nothing of which to be ashamed. *The righteous have no cause for secrecy, except in doing good.*

Except in doing good. It is often a recurrent theme in scripture *not to let the left hand know what the right hand is doing.* It is interesting to read that the only reason for secrecy should be in doing good things. We should not be boastful, or arrogant, or proud in displaying the good things we do. We should *do good,* but the good we do should be done in secret so we don't make others feel uncomfortable or obligated, so we aren't asking for praise, so the person doesn't outshine the deed.

Today I pray that the only secrets I keep will be secrets involved in doing good.

The Voice in our Souls

Do not the power, and goodness, and the justice of God reveal themselves in all nature? The panorama around us, the voice in our souls, they all speak of God. The Holy Quran, p. 1671

Autumn is definitely in the air; I can *smell* it this morning. It is in the blossoms from the flowering vine that have turned brown and gently flutter onto the veranda steps to be swept away with a swish of the broom. It is in the leaves from the kumquat tree that have fallen brown and brittle on the path, to be crushed and crunched under my sandal. It is in the hint of coolness in the morning air. *The power and goodness and justice of God reveal themselves in all nature.*

In the changing of the seasons I see the changes in myself. Another summer has passed, another autumn is on the threshold; winter is not far off. I look at my grandchildren for whom the seasons have shown the greatest change: the four year old is in pre-school, the two year old is quite verbal; the one year old is launching out by herself as she embarks on the adventure of walking! I look at myself as I climb all those stairs to the third floor to give class, not with quite the same spring to my step as there was last year. I am glad to be the age I am; it is right and good and natural to age – part of the cycle of nature. There is power and goodness and justice in the seasonal changes that take place in nature, and take place within my children and grandchildren, and within myself.

Autumn is definitely in the air – I can hear the voice in my soul speaking of God. Perhaps as I age, that voice becomes clearer, more distinct; perhaps it is only that *I am listening.* When the voice of my soul spoke when I was younger, perhaps I was too distracted by all the noise around me: the requests of children and spouse; the demands of students and co-workers; the dozens of voices that speak to one throughout the day, to really listen to what the voice of my soul was whispering. Now, I am more inclined to *listen.*

I often tell my children to *listen to the voice within that reminds them of how valued, how cared for and how loved they are.* I know the voice within their souls is whispering to their spirits of their value, of how cared for they are, of how loved they are! I know that Allah speaks to us, deep within our hearts, of how we are valued, and cared for and loved.

This morning I look at the panorama of nature around me: the flowers that are still in bloom; the flowers that are drying on the stem and will soon be tossed about by the wind; the leaves that are crushed and crunch under my feet as I sweep the steps and walk in front of the house; I look at the plot of garden where the bulbs of daffodils and iris sleep; it is dry and empty this morning, in Spring it will be ablaze with blooms: the *power and goodness and the justice of God is revealed in nature.* Everything happens in the time it is meant to happen.

This morning I think about my children and grandchildren and how daily they grow and change. I think about myself and how I daily grow older. It is all right. All is happening the way it is meant to happen. This morning I listen to the voice of God within my soul; it reassures me that my children and grandchildren are valued and cared for and loved; that I am valued, and cared for and loved. The voice within my soul reassures me that their lives, and my life are like the seasons, and that it is all good!

Today, I pray, I will hear the voice of my soul and heed what it says.

What Each Soul has Earned

Each soul will be paid out just what it has earned, without favor or injustice. Sura 3:25

I was in my last year of teaching high school English. For the first assembly at school, I gave a short history of the work of Quakers in Palestine. When I was thinking about what to say, I realized that I had come to the school before any of the students were born. When I thought some more, I realized that I had come to the school before many of their parents were born! When I thought even more, I realized that I had come to the school before 80% of the teachers were born, and of the remaining 20% who were born, only three of them were old enough to be in school. It certainly put things into perspective. *I was ancient.*

I can look back at all the years I have taught and wonder what I have to show for it. I don't own a car (I can walk to work.) I don't have central heating (but believe I *preserve* better in the cold). I don't have a dishwasher, or a microwave, or a vacuum cleaner, and only a semi-automatic washer (which I fill with buckets of water and watch as it agitates). I won't have a pension. I don't have piles of money in the bank, and almost never use a credit card. The house is furnished with cast-offs and dustbin finds. The curtains are hand-sewn on a hand-cranked machine, made from material bought from a place that sells flawed fabric by weight. The monetary worth of my material possessions is not much. I don't have much to leave my kids. I joke with them that when I die, they are just going to have to back a pick-up truck to the front door and start heaving. It probably is a good thing that we don't take anything with us; I'd be a bit embarrassed showing up at the Pearly Gates (if that's where I'm going) with my black canvas bag from Millers.

I can also look back at all the years I have taught and am amazed at the wonderful individuals who have touched my life! I remember all the students I taught and what joyful spirits they were. (I can add that to the positive side of my ledger.) It was through teaching that my *third child* came into my life. (I can certainly add that to the plus side of my account book.) I can look at my adult children, their spouses, the grandchildren and *know that my life has been blessed.* (I can add that to the balance in my ledger.) Looked at from that angle, I have had a rich and full life– and am really quite wealthy. I have always tried to be kind, and thoughtful, and considerate and generous and loving. I suspect it is really because people have been kind and thoughtful and considerate and generous and loving to me. I think my life has been blessedly rich in the things that are important. I pray that I have shared some of that *wealth* with others.

Each soul will be paid out just what it has earned.

Polishing the Heart's Lamp

Polishing the lamp of the heart. Wali Ali, <u>Essential Sufism,</u> p. 154

When I first moved to the Middle East one of the marks of a good homemaker was the shine on her pots. The pots and pans weren't just washed in hot, soapy water, but they were scoured with steel wool and olive oil soap, scoured so that, almost literally, you could see your image in them. Now that was polishing a pot!

When I first moved to the Middle East there were lots of household items made out of brass. There were brass planters, brass pitchers, brass trays, brass fingerbowls, brass lamps; everything rich in calligraphy cut in the brass. Everything needed polishing...and polishing the old-fashioned way: a cut lemon, salt, and a piece of old velvet. But once something was polished – it shone!

It did take a lot of rubbing and scouring and scrubbing and elbow grease to get the shine wanted; to get that special glow, to bring out the beauty or the mirror-reflection. It is much easier just to wash and wipe and call it done. It is clean. The item is serviceable. Who really cares if it is polished?

You remember the story of the genie and his lamp: you rub and rub and rub and then with a puff of magic smoke presto! – There's the genie to grant your wishes. If you don't polish the lamp, you don't see the genie, and you don't get the three wishes. Childhood fantasy? Of course, yet...

Like the pots and pans in my kitchen and the pieces of brass that accent the décor of the house, the lamps of our hearts need polishing. We don't polish them with a cut lemon, salt and a piece of old velvet. We don't polish them with pads of steel wool, olive oil soap and elbow grease. They are polished, often through pain and stress, heartache and sorrow – rubbed with raw emotion so they shine. They aren't scoured and scraped and scratched to peel away the grease and grime and tarnish. They are polished, often through the touch of a loved one, the kind words of a friend, the beauty of a sunrise, the peacefulness of a sunset, the feel of good, clean earth as we work in the garden, the knowledge that God is present – always, caring for us, guiding us, loving us. Allah polishes the lamps of our hearts in so many ways, so they glow and shine and illumine the darkness.

I am thankful that Allah polishes the lamp of my heart.

Existence and Joy

You carry all the ingredients to turn your existence into joy. Mix them! Mix them! "To Build a Swing," <u>The Gift: Poems by Hafiz the Great Sufi Master,</u> p.48

Sometimes we look at our existence and think: *Is this all there is?"* We are often burdened with the tedium of housework, toddlers, the seemingly same, dull routine. We are often frustrated with the traffic, the lack of a parking place, the moods of co-workers. We are often tired of the seemingly endless obligations, commitments, and demands on our time and energy. There are times when our existence seems anything *but* joyful.

We expect something from *outside of ourselves* to make our existence happier– perhaps even joyful. Perhaps if we hired a maid, the toddlers went to day care, there was some interruption to the dullness of the routine. Perhaps if the traffic was light, if we made all the green lights, we found an empty parking space near the door, and our co-workers were in a great mood. Perhaps if there weren't so many obligations, so many commitments, so many demands on our time and energy, we would have time to work in the garden, watch the game on TV, go to a boxing match, take a late evening walk with our spouse and kids. Perhaps if there really were something from *outside of ourselves to turn our existence into joy,* our lives would be different.

The truth is *we* carry all the ingredients to turn *our existence into joy inside us!* We can *choose* a mop that likes to dance! Put on some dancing music, waltz around the floor mopping, cleaning and dancing! We can *choose* to enjoy our toddlers as they stand on a chair, an apron tied under their arms, their small hands swishing the dishrag over the silverware. We can *choose* to use the time, waiting for the traffic to move, for the light to change, to listen to an audio-book or to sing along with the song on the radio. We can *choose* to be happy about the parking place at the extreme end of the parking lot, as we get in some free exercise as we hike to the office. We can *choose* to compliment our co-workers, to joke with them around the coffee pot, to smile at the customers upon whom we wait. We can *choose* to enjoy the company of cousins, and aunts and uncles and neighbors, and friends – thinking ourselves *blessed* that they are in our lives. We can *choose* to enjoy the demand on our time and energy as they are concrete evidence that we are *alive!* We can *choose* to be glad of the tiredness that comes at the end of a day – of the chance to cuddle with our spouse, thankful for the baby who snoozes contentedly in her crib. We can *choose* to turn our present existence into *joy!* We carry all the ingredients within us. All we need to do is: *Mix them! Mix them!*

I would pray that today I will be conscious that I carry all the ingredients within me to turn my present existence into joy. Today is the day I will *mix them!*

Making People Feel Good

Some people once asked Hazerti Ali, the son-in-law of the Prophet, how they might help others. They had no money or food to spare. He told them to smile at others, to do the best to make other people feel cared for. <u>Essential Sufism,</u> p. 18

Often we want to know how we can really help others. We are asked to donate money, to make contributions, to give out of our bounty. In the Christian tradition believers are encouraged to tithe one-tenth of their income; in Islam believers are encouraged to give *zakat,* at least a minimum of 2.5% of their income/savings; it is a blessing to give more. Believers are encouraged, no matter what their religious affiliation, to *share* whatever they have.

When the son-in-law of the Prophet was asked, by those who were poor, how they could help as they had no money or food to spare *he told them to smile at others, to do the best to make other people feel cared for.* How easy that is to do! To look someone in the eye, and to genuinely smile at them...acknowledge their existence at that moment in time...recognize their presence right then. It costs nothing to smile at the people we work with; it costs nothing to smile at the people we wait on; it costs nothing to put a smile in our voice when we are talking to someone on the phone; it costs nothing to stand at the door of our classroom and greet our students with a smile as they come into class. It costs so little to try our best to make other people feel cared for.

We tend to think of helping others in terms of *money.* We see ads on the television: *For a few cents a day you can feed a hungry child; your dollars will support a child in school.* Folks come to our door soliciting money for cancer research and the fireman --- good causes, and we give. We are encouraged to donate used clothes and toys to *Goodwill*; to do volunteer hours at a homeless shelter – all good causes. We hear of someone in need, and we organize fundraisers to help them out. *And it is right and good that we do.*

Financial help is important help, necessary help; practical help. It is our religious duty to share whatever we have. And we *all, probably, have more than we need.* In addition to whatever monetary help we can give, is the truth that we can *smile at others, do our best to make other people feel cared for.* We can do this every day, no matter where we are.

I try to think of ways to let my children know that they are valued, and *cared for* and loved. I try to think of ways to make the people who are often overlooked feel *cared for* ---the woman who makes the coffee at school and sweeps the floor; the secretaries in the office who are overworked and often not acknowledged for all they do; the guard at the gate, the gardener who dead-heads the flowers; the man with rotten teeth who comes once a month to sell me a pamphlet I can't read.

Today I will smile at those I meet; I will look for ways – however small they might be- to let others know they are cared for.

Everything Flows from God

If everything flows from God and everything returns to God, do you truly own anything? <u>Essential Sufism,</u> p.185

It is somewhat freeing to know that we truly don't own anything! When my in-laws died, and I moved into their house, I went through forty years of *things:* things that had belonged to my mother-in-law, things that had belonged to my father-in-law; things that had belonged to sisters-in-law; things that had belonged to my father-in-law's sister. The house was bulging with things that I suppose had had importance: things about which, at one time, was said: *this is mine.* They went to their graves with just the things they wore. In the end, they owned nothing. *If everything flows from God and everything returns to God, do we truly own anything?*

I have an aunt, through marriage, (really a second cousin of my wife's) who is waiting for death. She is eighty-six, senile, in need of round-the-clock care in order to survive. Someone must feed her, and bathe her, and dress her, and take her to the toilet. And thankfully, there *are* people devoted to her who are caring for her. She lives in what was once the grandest hotel in town. It is crammed with *things.* At one time she was thankful for the *things she owned.* Now, she is not even aware of the things around her. Upon her death, they will go to another, who for a brief period of time, will *own them.* Then they will pass on to another, or perhaps be sold at auction and for a brief period of time be *owned* by yet another. *If everything flows from God and everything returns to God, do we truly own anything?*

A distant cousin – a shirttail relative really – was visiting from the States. She was admiring the bits and pieces that furnish my home. Among them, at the time, was an antique sewing basket that had belonged to her great grandmother. It had been given to me by her great grandmother's daughter years before. When I saw her looking at it, fingering the straw thinking of a great grandmother she had never known, I decided to give her the basket. After all, it was only a *thing* – I thought it might give her pleasure to have something that once belonged to a woman, related, yet whom she had never known. If someone admires something in my home, I am likely to ask if they would like it – and give it to them. *Everything we have flows from God and everything returns to God, we don't truly own anything.*

It is somewhat freeing to know that we truly don't own anything because it also then means that *nothing material owns us.*

I would pray today for the realization that *everything flows from God and everything returns to God, and that I truly don't own anything.* How freeing that truth is!

Difficulties and Relief

With every difficulty there is relief. Sura 94:5

We look at the difficulties of our life and think: *there is no solution!* We look at the difficulties of our life and think: *things will always be this way.* We look at the difficulties of our life and think: *there will never be any relief.*

When I first became a single parent with young children to care for, I thought: *this is going to be my life---there will never be any relief to the loneliness, the despair, the feeling that I can't cope.* When I was first told that I needed brain surgery, and after the operation that I would never have use of my right hand, never walk without a cane, never speak clearly – I thought: *this is going to be my life – there will never be any relief from the frustration, the despair, the feeling that I couldn't cope.*

We look at our loved ones as they wrestle with drug addition, as their marriages seem to be going through a rough patch, as they struggle with raising preschoolers, their concern over medical problems. We feel with our loved ones as they deal with abrasive relatives, as they contend with irritating bosses, or intrusive co-workers. We look at the difficulties they have to face and wonder: *where is the relief?*

Yet, the truth is, *with every difficulty there **is relief.*** At first we may not see it; we may not recognize it; we may not acknowledge it, but it is there. God/Allah doesn't leave us without a solution for our difficulty. I can look back at the early days of single parenting and realize that God was always there, guiding me along the way. The loneliness was soon replaced with the joy of the children I was raising – there was comfort in hugging them before they went to bed; there was healing for despair in their laughter and smiles: there was the realization that *I could cope.* I have wonderful children, *proof that there was relief* from the difficulties I thought were so overwhelming.

I survived brain surgery. I did learn to walk without a cane; to use my right hand, to speak clearly – I went on to do intricate cross-stitch wall hangings for the weddings of my three children; to knit baby blankets and sweaters and booties for the children they had; I came to see the frustration and despair replaced with feelings of accomplishment, satisfaction; I came to acknowledge, with Allah's care and guidance, there *is relief for every difficulty.* All marriages go through rough patches ---and if we stick to it, and work at it, there *is relief.* Almost magically, one day our preschoolers are off to school, they no longer will present the same challenges and we will rejoice in the wonderful individuals they have become. Medical problems can be addressed, abrasive relatives can be dealt with kindly and sensitively; irritating bosses and intrusive co-workers also have their struggles, and we can endeavor to see beyond the surface as we realize that they are struggling too. For every difficulty *there is relief.*

God's Generosity

We must thank God. For if God had not wished it so, we would not have been here; you would not have been here, we would not have met. It is God's generosity that we are here and that we are together. <u>Essential Sufism,</u> p.18

I know that Allah has written people into our lives. I know that it is not just by chance that we are born into our families. I know that it is not just by chance that we are drawn to the individuals who become our spouses. I know that the children who slip into our lives and hearts are put there by God; I know that it isn't just by chance. I thank God that He has wished it so. *It is God's generosity that we are here and that we are together.*

I look at the individuals whom I love, and I *know* that Allah has written them into my life for a reason and that I am richly blessed that He has wished it so. I *know* that it is *God's generosity that we are here and that we are together.*

I think before each baby is born, Allah plans whom to entrust with this little one. I think He knows who will make the perfect parents to care and nurture and love this precious spirit. I don't think it is ever a mere matter of chance. I look at my grandchildren and I *know* they are with the parents they are meant to be with. They are with the parents who will deal with their stubbornness, their creative mischief, their hiding the *"o"* key from the laptop. They are with the parents who will love them in spite of their spells of naughtiness; in spite of the sleepless nights, even when they are challenging and questioning and in *their terrible twos.* They are with the parents who will *love them forever and always-* just like the line from a bedtime story.

I know that God has written a third child into my life. He is now no longer a child, but a man fully grown with children to love and, *inshallah-* God willing, many-children-yet-to-be. I thank God every day for His generosity in *that we are here and that we are together.* I know that we would not have been here; we would not have met, if Allah had not wished it to be so.

I know that Allah has written people into our lives. I know that it is not just by chance that we are with the people we are with. I know that it is not just by chance that we love the people whom we love. I know that it is not just by chance that Allah has placed in our hearts the individuals He has planted there. *It is God's generosity that we are here and that we are together.* And I praise God for His wisdom and His blessing.

The Depths of Darkness

From the depths of darkness, He will lead them forth into light. Sura 2:257

I stood in a crowd of hundreds today in popular support for the proposal to be brought before the United Nations asking that Palestine be recognized as a sovereign state. I listened to the rhetoric of the speakers; I listened to the patriotic music being played in the background; I listened to the crowd sing the national anthem of Palestine. I listened to the hope and I was touched.

I looked at the crowd: men in business suits, school girls in their uniforms, women carrying babies. Some in the crowd I recognized: doctors, lawyers, professionals, butchers, grocery store owners; the crippled boy who sells newspapers out of a baby buggy. I looked as Palestinian flags were waved in the breezeless sun. I listened as the crowd cheered and clapped and sang. I listened to the hope and I was touched.

For almost seven decades the Palestinians have lived in the shadows- have been in the depths of political darkness in spite of the sun on the Palestinian hills. I thought, perhaps – just perhaps – they will be lead forth into the light. Perhaps it won't be right now- perhaps we will struggle along a bit more in the darkness- but eventually *He will lead us forth into light!*

There are times in our lives when we seem to live and linger in the depths of darkness. Nothing seems to go as we would wish it would go; prayers are answered, but not in the way we would wish them answered; dreams are fulfilled, but not as we had envisioned them fulfilled; we seem to grope in the dark without a light.

But the promise is there: *from the depths of darkness, He will lead them forth into light.* That gives me hope. Allah knows the darkness in which I move. And He is there to lead me forth into the light. He knows the shadows through which I stumble. And He is there to lead me forth into the light. He knows the night through which I crawl. And He is there to lead me forth into the light.

That is the message of this day: in whatever darkness we move, God is there to lead us forth into the light!

One's Own Death

Thinking about one's own death is an exercise in becoming more aware of one's present experiences. Essential Sufism, p. 28

I have been thinking about my own death a lot the last few days. This is probably due to the fact I have been visiting an aunt who is eighty-six, senile, has to be fed and dressed, taken to the pot, can't talk, can't see too well, and wears adult diapers. Then on Tuesdays I see a former colleague who lives six days a week in a nursing home, one day she comes to town to run errands: I go to carry her bags to the bus as she can't walk five steps without having to stop and catch her breath. Yesterday I received the copy of an obituary for a former classmate and it read like it had been written for a saint. (It made me contemplate writing my own obituary and sending it to my daughter to file away for that *inevitable moment. Sparkling, glowing,* definitely *not me.* One should be thankful that death, blessedly, tends to blur some of the reality.)

Because I have been thinking about my own death the last few days, I have been more aware of my *present.* When we realize, at some level, that we only have so many years, or months, or days, or hours, or minutes, or seconds, things do seem to run into a perspective of sorts. We tend to prioritize what we are doing and to think about what *really matters.* Of course, those I love *matter,* and this means that I feel almost compelled to *tell them* that they are loved – daily! Of course, it is important to not really let anger be the last thing that someone sees or hears from me --- after all *this may be the last time I see them or they hear me.* Of course, it doesn't really matter if the pillows are fluffed, or if there is an unwashed cup in the sink, or if the hangers in the closet are all facing the same direction, or if the rose bush has been dead-headed.

As I have been thinking about my own death the last few days, I am thinking about *how I want to be remembered.* I would like to be remembered for being kind, and thoughtful, and caring and funny. I would like to be remembered for being accepting and tolerant and not critical. I would like to be remembered for greeting people with a smile and sometimes a hug. I would like to be remembered for the little things that have made someone feel loved. If that is how I wish to be remembered, that is *how I need to live my present.*

I thought about my own death when I climbed the fifty stairs to my classroom in the attic. I had come to the conclusion that I should be thankful, as I was really *fifty steps closer to heaven.* And blessedly, my classroom wasn't in the basement where I would have been that much closer to feeding the fires of hell! Thinking about death demands that we are more aware of the present, as the moment - the present - this second is all we really have.

I would pray that today I will be conscious, yes, of my own inevitable death, only in that it will help me be aware of how I should be acting in the present.

All One Put Forward

That Day will Man be told all that he put forward, and all that he put back. Sura 75:13

There was a popular movie some years ago around the theme of *paying things forward* ---of doing good deeds, performing thoughtful acts, of going out of one's way for another. There was no expectation of reward, just the hope that the person would do a good deed for the next person; that they would *pay it forward*.

In the Quran it speaks of the Day of Judgment when all of one's deeds ---good or not-so-good – will be weighed. It tells that on that day, *man will be told all that he put forward, and all that he put back.* There will be a record of each act, each thought, each feeling. The times when we are thoughtful, and kind, and generous, and giving; the times when we are selfish, and unkind, and miserly, and begrudging – all will be in a record that is read to us. The good things that we *put forward,* and the not-so-good things that we *put back* will be revealed.

The concept that one's actions and deeds are known is a powerful idea. If we know we are being observed, we seem to endeavor to *be good.* If we think we are being unobserved, there is the temptation to sometimes be *not-so-good.*

I guess I need reminding that God *does* see everything!

Softening the Heart

A kind word or glance softens the heart, and every hurtful word or act closes or hardens the heart. Sheik Muzaffer, Essential Sufism, *p.35*

I was recently at a hall where people were coming to offer their condolences. In the hall the men and women sat in separate sections. The men visited with the men, and the women visited with the women. There was an older woman who came in. She was dressed in traditional, conservative dress and her head was swathed in a long white shawl. I glanced at her as she passed. I had known her when she was a young woman and probably hadn't seen her in almost thirty years.

When she came to leave, she walked through the men's line of mourners. When she got to me, she stopped and shook my hand, and we spoke for a few seconds. As she was going out the door and down the steps, I left the men's line and called after her. I took her hand and said that I wanted her to know how much she had meant to the woman who had died. I told her how the woman had often spoken about her, of how she always, in her heart, loved her as a daughter. The woman cried and said: *I loved her like a mother too. In fact I lived longer with her than I did with my own mother. I am so glad you told me this!* I was so glad I told her too. *A kind word or glance softens the heart.*

The last few months the faces and names of people I have known in the past have been popping into my mind. These reminders seem to be prompts for me to contact these individuals and tell them how much they meant to me at a particular point in my life. I have emailed several, and even though I have received few replies, I still think it was the right thing to do: people need to be reminded of how much they meant to someone.

I have also in the last few months found hurtful words whispering to my mind when I think of folks who somehow have hurt me, or ignored me, or made me feel less than what I am. In my mind I have *said* words that I would never actually say to them. I realize that these hurtful words have *hardened my heart*. I want to be better than this.

I *want* to have a soft heart; I want to say the kind word and give the kind glance: I don't want my heart to be hardened by hurtful words or acts. I would pray this day, that I would say kind words and give kind glances to those I meet.

Allah's Blessings

Allah's blessings will be more than the merits of men. <u>The Glorious Koran</u>, p. 1671

When we pause to think, the blessings of Allah are without number. They are the little things that seem to punctuate the sentences of our day and remind us of the goodness and blessings of God. There are the buds on the rose bush in its earthen pot. There are the shoots that are just breaking the soil – a promise of a blossom yet-to-be. There is the unexpected invitation to dinner, just when you have taken a fresh, pear pie out of the oven – a perfect dessert to take with you. There is the unexpected email in your inbox, connecting you to a friend from the past. There is the warmth of a room filled with the discarded treasures of others. There are the *little things* – of no consequence really – that are gentle reminders of Allah and His care for us.

The blessings are *always* there but we are sometimes caught in the busy-ness of the day and fail to see them. We concentrate rather on the frustrations, the little irritations, the distractions that seem to cloud our sight and blind us to the blessings.

In the inbox this morning was an email from a friend. In the email she was recounting that she had visited an old friend who had just had her second leg amputated -- a consequence of diabetes. During my power-walk this morning, a blister on one toe burst and added an element of discomfort to my walk. I kept walking, enduring the mild shoots of pain, and thought – *it is a blessing that I can feel the discomfort; I am really blessed to be able to make this morning walk.*

I have lived for over forty years in the Middle East. I have come to appreciate and value the philosophy that everything is a blessing from God – even those things that don't seem to be blessings at the time. I appreciate and value the almost automatic response: *illhumdillah or nush'kur Allah* (thank God, praise God) when asked: *How are you?* As a child, I can remember by mother saying when something bad happened: *It is probably a blessing in disguise.*

Throughout my life, I have found that to be true. Allah continues to bless us, even when we think we are not being blessed. It isn't as though we *deserve* the blessings, or have *earned* the blessings, that they are ours through *merit.* They are there because Allah loves us. He blesses our days, as a loving father would wish to bless the days of his children.

Allah's blessings will be more than the merits of men. I *know* that that is true.

Open your eyes to the blessings that Allah has given you this day.

Our Spiritual Destiny

The greatest news for man is his spiritual destiny; listen to the voice in your soul. <u>The Glorious Quran,</u> p. 1671

For each of us there is an inner voice that whispers to our conscience that allows us to see and realize the truth, free of the camouflage of bias and prejudice, of propaganda and religious dogma, of politics and crippling custom. But we have to *listen to that voice* within our soul.

All people, no matter what their religious or cultural tradition, no matter what their ethnic or racial group, no matter what their political affiliation, have a *spiritual destiny.* We are all, in a true sense, children of God. We may have different, diverse identities, but we are all the same at the core. We love our children and families; we want to be happy and successful; we want to be healthy and good; we want to be safe – free from fear, free from poverty, free from war and the rumors of war. We have a *spiritual destiny.*

God *wants* us to get along. He *wants* us to see the brother, the sister, the child, the parent in another. God *wants* me to realize that the person I see is basically *just like me.* God *wants* us to *listen to the voice in our souls.*

Sometimes the voice in my soul speaks so softly that in the clamor of the day I am deaf to its sound. Sometimes the voice in my soul speaks loudly enough that I can hear it clearly. I have to train myself to *listen* to what the voice is saying. *Always* I am better when I listen to the voice within.

I believe God speaks to our spirits. I believe that there is a voice in our soul guiding us. I am destined to *see that of God* in each person I meet. I am destined to *listen to the voice in my soul* when it whispers to my heart how I should be.

Eternal Life

In the sojourn of this life we must respond to Allah's hand in fashioning us...we must be ready for our departure into the life that will be eternal. Sura 6:48

On the piano, amid the collection of framed photos, there is one of a little boy, just a year old. He is all dressed up for the photographer: white shirt, white shorts, white socks, and white shoes. His hair, what there is of it, has been combed into soft, black curls. He is smiling, showing four teeth, and dimples, probably at the instructions of the photographer or his mother to: *Smile! Smile!*

On the bookcase in the bookroom, there is another photo of a twenty-one year old. His black hair is wavy. He is wearing black, horn rimmed glasses; he is smiling closed mouth, but the dimples still show. In the sitting room, behind the door, is a framed, life-size charcoal drawing of the same man: gone is the wavy black hair; he is bald with a white fringe; he is sporting a white goatee; the horned-rimmed glasses have been replaced with frameless lenses; the smile is the same; there are still the dimples.

The child in the photo was in and out of hospitals the first five years of his life. The doctors never quite knew what the problem was. At the age of six, there was an exploratory operation. The little boy was made *backwards* inside. The operation re-arranged the insides.

The young man in the photo on the bookshelf was traveling abroad for the first time. He was stepping into a different, foreign culture – foreign for him. The adjustment was not easy. He made mistakes;

he struggled; he learned. He eventually married a girl from the culture into which he had stepped. After nine years of marriage, she died leaving behind their two children to rear.

The charcoal drawing, drawn from a photo, was a gift marking his retirement from a teaching job he had held for 45 years. Twelve years ago he was operated on for what was thought to be a brain tumor. It was discovered, that not only had he been made *backwards* inside, he had, from birth a small hole in his head. It was corrected.

None of our lives are easy. Each soul has a tale to tell, a story to weave. Life is seldom as we expect it to be, or would wish it would be. We travel onwards stage by stage, infant, child, adolescent, young person, mature adult. We are a child, a newly married person, a parent, a grandparent. We are actively employed; we are retired.

I have found, in all the stages of my life that God/Allah has been there. Even, perhaps most importantly, He has been there when I thought He was not.

Man's life is never easy; it seems that we never really rest. I rejoice that as we travel our journeys, Allah is there – as He has always been.

110

True Wealth

True wealth is a state in which you do not crave anything that you do not already have. <u>Essential Sufism,</u> 180

When my children were little, and they didn't really know any better, I always told them that we were *independently wealthy*. I worked at a poverty-level job, didn't own a car, lived in a house furnished with the bits and pieces of other folks' homes, bought the children's underwear and pajamas from cardboard boxes on the street, and if a Christmas toy required batteries, I bought the batteries for the next Christmas. Yet, we were *independently wealthy*.

We had plenty to eat; we had plenty to read; we played lots of board games and such. Everything we needed we had. Fortunately, we lived in a town where we didn't need a car. There was adequate, and cheap, public transportation. We also *walked a lot*. Fortunately, we lived in a part of the world where, at the time, there weren't malls, and shopping centers, and amusement parks, and such. The television broadcasted only certain hours a day, and there were only two channels. Fortunately, there weren't any fast-food chains, but I made homemade pizza, homemade hamburgers and French fries, homemade donuts.

We didn't have central heating, or air conditioning, or a microwave, not even a vacuum cleaner. Yet, we were *independently wealthy*. The kids were raised not having much when it came to things. They had books, they had games, they had music, they had friends, they had relatives. All that they really needed they had.

True wealth is a state in which you do not crave anything that you do not already have.

It is so easy to get caught up in wanting *things.* There is almost this *craving* for more, for better, for the latest, for the most expensive. I still use a wrist watch that I have had for about fifteen years. I occasionally need to replace the battery and the plastic strap. It is functional; it keeps accurate time. I must confess, that at times I *do* have the urge for things – things I can find in dumpsters, things that others have tossed that I can repaint, recover, re-do, re-use. In reality though, there is nothing I want or need that I do not already have – and already have a *number of.* In that sense, I suppose I am *wealthy.*

I don't have a lot of money in the bank, or squirreled under the mattress, or stuffed in the teapot. I seem to always have enough though, enough to supply my needs and more than my needs.

I think that true wealth is a state of mind. It is the realization that we do not need anything more than what we already have. We probably have more than what we really need, and certainly enough to share with others.

You and I are probably really quite wealthy and really need nothing more than what we have.

Impatience

If we are impatient, we are no longer in the present; we are busy with the future that has not yet come. <u>Essential Sufism,</u> p. 183

Patience is certainly *not* one of the virtues I possess. Of the many people I know, I am probably one of the most *impatient.* It is easy for me to expect things I want to happen, to happen *now – right at this moment.*

The spinner on my semi-automatic washer stopped spinning. I was at the repair shop at 8 in the morning getting my name and telephone number on the list. I planned to be home all day to await the call and the repairman. I waited and waited and waited, growing more impatient with the movement of the hands on the clock. My mind would play over certain scenarios: *This is the third time the spinner hasn't worked. I'll probably have to buy a new washer. Yesterday it was the computer; today the washer; tomorrow probably the TV or refrigerator.* I didn't even go outside to take out the trash for fear I would *miss the repairman's call.* Finally at 4:30 I thought, *Well, I guess it will be tomorrow. I hate to waste another day at home just waiting.*

I tried to talk myself into being patient, whispering to my mind: *You don't really need a spinner. It is probably better for you to wring clothes by hand anyway. If you do decide to buy a new machine, semi-automatics are really not that expensive. The repairman is really reliable, you've used him for years; he'll show up tomorrow.*

The entire day I was living a future that hadn't come yet; I hadn't been in the present the whole day. At 4:30 I sat in the rocker on the veranda with a book I was finishing and a cup of coffee. Just as I sat down the phone rang. It was the repairman and he was on his way.

He took one look at the machine. He rotated the spinner with his hand a couple of times. He tested it with two wet bath towels and it worked fine. He was here, literally, about ten minutes. I joked with him that the machine had *missed his visits* and had put on the pretense of not working. I had already been *purchasing a new machine* in my mind, and in reality he reluctantly took $20 for his visit.

This was just a simple example, but how often do we get really impatient over things of which we really have no control. We imagine the worst scenario possible. We seem to live patches of our lives in a future that hasn't come yet, and which perhaps will never be as we imagine it. How often do we fail to really live in the present?

It was only 5:15 this morning when I came through the black, iron gate after my power-walk. A big, round yellow moon was still pinned to the sky. I had been thinking of all I wanted to do today, of what I wanted to write, of the shopping I wanted to do, of what to fix for lunch, of who to visit in the afternoon – then I looked up and saw the moon. I paused and said out loud, *Thank you God for this present moment.*

The Rewards of Service

The rewards of service are not to be measured by immediate results, but occur in countless hidden ways of patience and restraint. Be strong against evil, but kind and gentle among yourselves: the seed will grow and become strong to your wonder and delight. (Quran p. 1390)

The pre-dawn morning call to prayer slips through my sleep. It is a morning of Ramadan, the month of fasting. From dawn to dusk the faithful are to refrain from food and drink. It is to be a time of remembering the poor, the unfortunate, the hungry. It is a time of remembering Allah's blessings. It is a time of reading through the Quran, of being more faithful in one's prayer life.

The faithful are reminded of the need of purifying their words and *thoughts*. It is a month when one is more aware of the need of *self-restraint,* the need of curb *all* of one's appetites– not just the appetite for food and drink, but the appetite for gossip, for feeding's one's pleasures, for gnawing on the bones of resentment.

Ramadan is a time when one should become more *aware* of the needs of others and the paths they walk. Everyone's road is marked with pot holes and ruts; no one's journey is always smooth. Sometimes we get so absorbed in our own journey that we fail to recognize the journey of others and acknowledge the difficulties they may be having.

The month of Ramadan is a time when one should be more aware of the people they encounter. A time when one should silently send a *prayer* their way that Allah will bless them. It is a time when one should be generous in anonymously giving to those in need; it is a time of *sharing* whatever one has.

Ramadan is a time when one strives to be his or her best self; the kind of person he/she was *meant to be;* the kind of person Allah *wants* him/her to be!

Being a Burden

Do not be a burden to others. Al Ghazzali <u>Essential Sufism</u>

A collage of framed photos hangs above the piano in my sitting room. One photo– taken in 1907– is a family group photo. In the center of the faded photograph there is an old woman in native dress holding a baby. The baby is my mother-in-law; the old woman is her grandmother, *Sitti Henneh. Sitti Henneh* lived to be 106 and was still practicing her skill as a midwife when she was 102.

My mother-in-law used to tell the story of how she could hear her grandmother praying every night that God would take her when there was *still dust on her feet.* She wanted to be active, still involved, not a *burden to anyone.*

No one *wants* to be a burden to others. All of us *want* to be independent until the end – and hope to just *slip into heaven with the dust still on our feet.*

As my friends and I age, more and more talk about *who will take care of us* pops up in conversations. Friends who have remained unmarried or childless begin to wonder if they have made the *right* decisions about remaining unmarried and not having *children to care for them.* Those of us who did marry, and do have children, don't want to *live in our children's back pockets.* Almost always in the conversations the comment is made: *I don't want to be a burden.*

But there *is* a difference in being *cared for* and in *being a burden.* I am reminded of an old film I once saw. The film was about orphans and based on the story of Father Flanagan and Boys Town. One clip sticks in my mind. It was of an older boy carrying his little brother. When asked if it wasn't a burden for him, he replies: *He ain't heavy; he's me brother.*

Perhaps it boils down to love and *attitude-* the attitude of the caregiver and the attitude of the one needing care. No one wants to be a burden, or wants to feel burdened. We each need to think about how the other might be feeling, but there is blessing for others in allowing them to care for us.

My prayer would be that I would *die with the dust still on my feet,* and that I would be a burden to no one.

Real Peace

The only real peace comes from faith in God. Essential Sufism

Faith – the belief in the *unseen, the unexplainable.* We plant a seed in the ground and have faith that it will burst open, send out tender shoots and grow. We become parents and have faith that the child we are given to love and nurture will grow into a healthy, happy, successful, vibrant individual. We choose a life-partner and have faith that happiness will be ours; that we will always be together. We embark on a new career and have faith that we will flourish and prosper. *Faith* in our minds is perhaps synonymous with *hope.*

But *faith* and *hope* are not synonymous. The word *hope* seems to contain the element of *doubt.* In *faith* the element of doubt is absent. Faith is the *certainty* that the best will happen– *faith* that God cares for us, watches out for us, and wants only our good.

One of the most positive beliefs in Islam is the belief that *everything from Allah is good* –even those things which, at the time, may seem anything but good! God *knows* what we need; God loves us; God wants what is best for us. In *that* realization there is peace– peace in the certainty that whatever happens to us– *God is there!* Even if we do not *understand the why,* we have peace in the belief that *God is there* and therefore it is ultimately good. This *is faith!*

Some days we are plagued with restlessness and worry. We convince ourselves that things are *not going* to work out: we will not be successful in our new job; we will miss our connecting flight, we will never curb our little one's stubbornness, the test results will be positive, things will *always be the way they are right now—* there are a thousand and one things to worry about.

If after each statement we said *inshallah—* God willing, how different our attitude would be. *We will be successful in our new enterprise, inshallah. We will make our connecting flight, inshallah. Our little one will outgrow his stubbornness, inshallah. Things will not always be the way they are today, inshallah.* The belief that things will be *as they are meant to be* can bring real peace to our hearts. This *is faith!*

I *do* believe that *the only real peace comes from faith in God.*

What One Owes

To Allah he owes his life and all its blessings. <u>The Holy Quran</u>

Sitting here this early morning, thinking of life and its blessings, I am reminded of a hymn from my Methodist childhood: *Count Your Blessings*. I can still remember the first line: *When upon life's billows you are tempest tossed, when you are discouraged, thinking all is lost, Count your many blessings, name them one by one, And it will surprise you what the Lord hath done.*

Who among us has not been tempest tossed, discouraged, and thought that all is lost? All of us. Who among us has not, at least figuratively, *beaten our breast, sighed: 'woe is me'*, and gone through periods where life seemed *blessing-less* and we have wondered: 'why me?' All of us.

I can remember gym class as a child. I can still almost *smell* the red shorts and white t-shirt that had been in the gym bag a tad too long. I can painfully remember always being chosen last, and can still hear my mother saying: *Perhaps it is a blessing in disguise.* How could *always* being last be a blessing? Years later, as a teacher, I was able to sympathize with those who had to struggle a bit. That early experience *had* been a blessing in disguise.

Being the youngest, and though a boy, I was taught to clean house, cook, iron and the fundamentals of sewing and knitting. Mother's philosophy was: *It is better to know how and not have to, than to have to and not know how. You'll find it is a blessing in disguise.* Years later, when I became a single parent with young children, I recognized the *blessings* in that early training. I was prepared to keep a clean house, cook good meals, iron sheets and knit the kids' sweaters. That early training *had* been a blessing in disguise.

Not all of life's blessings are hidden, in fact, most are not. They are right there in plain sight; we just have to *see them:* the beauty of a flowering garden, the smile of a little one as she tosses *Cheerios* off her highchair tray, the joy of a toddler who slips his/her hand into yours as you cross the street, the love that shines out of the eyes of your spouse, the email that comes saying: *I was just thinking about you,* a sink free of dishes and newly scoured, putting your feet up and watching a match on TV, reading a good book - the list is endless. It is not just the 'big blessings' like recovery from brain surgery or breast cancer, or a 'near-death' experience, but the 'little blessings that punctuate our days.

Life is bursting with blessings. And they all come from God: *To Allah we owe our life and all its blessings.*

May you *see* the blessings that punctuate your life.

How the Good Suffer

*And you wonder how the good suffer and the evil thrive;
remember the final goal when all adjustments will be made.*
<u>The Holy Quran</u>

Bad things **do** seem to happen to good people. The good **do** seem
to suffer while the not-so-good seem to prosper. Sometimes it
seems the deserving never get a break, while the not-so-deserving
seem to thrive. These seem to be realities we can't ignore.

History is crammed with atrocities committed by truly *evil*
individuals who occupy lands, murder innocents, rape, pillage, and
destroy; individuals who uproot people, create refugees, practice
genocide, push drugs, lie, cheat, and steal and for a time seem to
prosper. Sometimes it *does* seem to be true that the *good suffer
and the evil thrive.*

How often have we heard, or thought, or said: *One day they will get
what they deserve!* We are not usually referring to the good who
suffer, but to the not-so-good. We *want* those who do *evil* to *pay*;
we certainly don't want them to reap any worldly benefit for being
bad.

Most religions teach some version of a *heavenly reward* for being
good; some kind of *heavenly equalization; the first shall be last and
the last shall be first.* Most religions seem to teach a belief that the
evil may thrive for a time on earth, but one day they will find
themselves in hell and be *shoveling coal for eternity.* They will get
what they deserve. The good will lay in lush gardens where crystal,

clear water eternally flows, and the evil will be served scalding water filled with pus. Evil may thrive for a bit, but it doesn't thrive in heaven! In heaven the good no longer suffer and *they* are the ones who thrive. That is what we are taught, isn't it?

I don't know why bad things happen to good people. I don't know why it seems that the evil thrive. I *do* believe that all conditions are temporary. I *do* believe that God sees everything and that there is ultimate justice; that every good deed is divinely remembered and recorded, and every evil act is also remembered and recorded. I *do* believe that there is a final *adjustment* when the tallies are made of each individual's life. We are accountable for our acts, and so are others! Good will be recognized and rewarded, and evil will be acknowledged and punished.

The truth is that God is loving and *just.*

Blind to the Light that Guides

Allah's laws must be obeyed; it is man's loss if he is deaf to the voice which teaches him, or blind to the light which guides him. <u>The Holy Quran</u>

There are simple rules of living: *be kind, thoughtful, thankful* and *honest.* If we don't follow these four simple guides who is the real loser? We are. When we were children our parent(s) probably told us to *'play nice', to tell the truth, to say 'thank you',* and to *share.* Our teachers at school, preachers at church, rabbis at temple, *Imams* at the mosque— all probably told us, through stories from religious texts and life experiences, to be: *kind, thoughtful, thankful* and *honest.* The voices were certainly there; sometimes we heard; sometimes we seemed to have wax in our ears.

Recently I saw a picture on the internet of an anonymous policeman putting new shoes on a barefoot homeless man. The picture glaringly said: *Be kind. Be thoughtful.* This past summer I tried to track down a former classmate— a woman I hadn't seen in almost fifty years. At the post office in the little, rural community in which she lived I learned that I had just missed her and her retarded daughter by ten minutes. The post mistress directed me to her house, but said 'she's living in a motel room until the State finds her new accommodations.' I stood in front of her home and talked to the neighbor lady. Some of the windows were broken; the rain spouting hung down from the roof in places; the front door had been nailed shut. The neighbor woman said that the woman was a widow; her one daughter lived 'Out West'; her retarded daughter was mean; and her only son 'lived at the bar.' It made me sad, but ironically, it also made me *thankful*; it made me *aware* and *appreciative* of all the blessings I had and often didn't *see*.

Recently I was visiting with old friends whom I had not seen in some time. They were commenting on the actions of a neighbor man. It would have been *convenient* to have agreed with their negative belief about the man, but I knew a different side of the story. I felt I had to be *honest* and to 'tell the truth' as I knew it to be.

It is not always *easy* to be honest. Sometimes it seems to be a *kindness* to *stretch* the truth a bit– to tell *white lies.* But in the long run, whom do we trust? Those we know to occasionally *stretch the truth*, or those who will be *honest*?

I don't want to be *deaf to the voice which teaches me,* or *blind to the light which guides me.* I want to be: *kind, thoughtful, thankful, honest* and most importantly *aware.* May we *hear* and *see* clearly. May we obey God's teaching and guidance.

God and Trust

Nothing will happen to us except what God has preordained for us. He is our Protector; in God the believers put all their trust. Sura 9:51

There is assurance in the belief that *nothing will happen to us except what is preordained.* There is security in the knowledge that God is our protector and can be *trusted.* There is safety in the awareness that *no matter what happens in our lives, God is there!*

Perhaps it is a bit *simplistic* and *naïve* to hold to the belief that *no matter what happens, this is what God wants!* We have a bad day at work— *Is this what God wanted?* We get caught in a traffic jam— *Is this what God wanted?* We go bald and get dark blemishes on our head — *this was preordained?* It's absurd to think this is all part of some *Divine Plan,* isn't it? Is it a bit *too simplistic — too naïve* to believe that bad days, traffic jams, and male-pattern baldness can be attributed to God?

There *is* a philosophy that says one can't appreciate the good days at work *unless* there are bad days at work; that one can't really appreciate clear roads with not a car in sight *unless* one is occasionally caught in a traffic jam; and that some men are really quite handsome when they are bald and purposely shave their heads! It all goes back to *how we choose to view* what is happening. I *choose* to believe that God is aware of even these very minor happenings in our lives, and that they are all okay— *part of a Divine*

Plan. Maybe they are; maybe they aren't. The important thing for me is the unshakeable belief that no matter what– God is there.

I am *sure* that in the major happenings in my life God has looked out for me. Through my wife's death, I became a single father when the children were quite young. The children are now grown, mature, successful, *grounded,* a joy to those around them and to me. In their memories of their mother she is always young, vivacious, and funny. Perhaps it *was written* for her to graduate from college, travel, marry, have children, and return to God when she had accomplished all she was meant to accomplish. I *choose* to believe and *trust* that God loved her as he loves my children and me. I don't *understand*, but I *believe.*

God *is* our Protector. We *can* put all our trust in Him. We *can* believe that *nothing will happen to us except what God has preordained*– we may not always *understand* – but we can always be confident that He loves us.

The Permanent Record

The pen is the symbol of the permanent record. <u>The Holy Quran</u>

We use a pen every day. We use it to sign checks, credit card receipts, contracts, licenses. We use a pen to fill out applications, declaration cards on a plane, answer questionnaires. We use a pen to make notes, scribble lists, do crossword puzzles, and doodle. There are ballpoint pens, dry-ink pens, fountain pens, felt-tip pens, and pens used for calligraphy. Man has always needed a pen to record the events that mark his life and the thoughts that fill his head. The pen is a *tool*; it is also a *symbol* of where man has been, what man has done, what man has thought.

In Islam, *the pen is the symbol of the permanent record.* Islam teaches that two angels are assigned to each person. The one angel, sitting on his/her right shoulder, keeps a record of all his/her good deeds. The second angel, sitting on the left shoulder, keeps an account of all his not-so-good deeds. It is hoped that the angel on the right should have a lot of writing to do and that the angel on the left shoulder can doze off with only an *occasional* deed to record.

In Islam it is believed that on Judgment Day each soul will be handed the *permanent record* that has been kept by these two angels. (One would hope the record of good deeds is pages longer than the record of bad deeds.) Based on what has been recorded, according to the Quran, the person will be assigned to *hell's fire* or to *gardens beneath which rivers flow.*

It is a bit sobering to think that *everything* we have ever done has been recorded; that *no* action is forgotten; that every unkind word, unkind deed, unspoken thought has been written down. It is a bit sobering to realize that every lie and deceitful act is *remembered and recorded!* It is a bit sobering to be held accountable for everything we did; that we can't hit the delete key and erase the history. But it is also reassuring to know that every kind word, kind deed, truthful word, and generous act is also recorded in a permanent record. It would behoove us, so it seems, to live a life punctuated with good words and deeds.

We live in an age that relies on some form of verifiable truth: written records, signatures on deeds/contracts, video tapes, voice recordings, pictures – things that will prove to those in authority - *if we were taken to court or arrested* –that we are honest and innocent. We want to be able to prove who we are, what we have or haven't done, and to what we are entitled.

Some things we purposely don't write down – things we would like to forget. It is almost as though *if there is no record, the deed never happened.* To think that *everything* we have said and done is written in a *permanent record* kept with God shakes us into wanting to do, and be, good.

Almost every time I use a pen, I think about that.

The Gate to Heaven

Even if we opened to them a gate to Heaven and they were to continue ascending therein; yet they would say: Our sight is confused as in drunkenness. Sura 15:14-15

I love this image! There is a gate open to Heaven; there are stairs leading to that gate; we are *actually climbing the stairs*– yet we don't believe it and think: 'I must be drunk.' There is also that voice of frustration over our failure to see the open gate, to *realize* we could be climbing the stairs; the failure to believe– *even though it is right there before our very eyes*– it can be true. It's a version of: *I see it, but I don't believe it.*

One line of poetry that I remember from my youth is: *Earth's crammed with Heaven and every common bush aflame with God. But only he who sees takes off his shoes; the rest sit round and pluck blackberries.* I can't recall the poet's name, but I have never forgotten the line, Earth *is* crammed with Heaven, but often we are too busy, too distracted, too blinded to see. It's as though we are going through life with blinders on, or those little black masks that are passed out on airplanes so one can sleep. At the very least, it is as though we have shades on; we may look cool, but our vision is tinted.

I am sure God gets frustrated with us at times. I can almost hear Him saying this line; *Even if we opened a gate to Heaven; even if man was actually ascending the stairs, he would still think that he must be confused as though he were drunk.*

We sometimes need that proverbial *brick wall to fall on us.*

The gates to Heaven *are* open; we *can* climb the stairs. *Earth is crammed with Heaven.* It is up to us to *see,* to take off our shoes, and not just sit around and *pluck blackberries.*

Lines for Meditation

Lines from the Quran

Would you be taught the steep path? It is to ransom the captive, to feed the hungry, the kindred, the orphans, and him *whose mouth is in the dust.* Sura 40:12-17

* * * * * * * *

He it is who ordains the night as a garment and sleep for rest, and ordains the day for waking up the soul. Sura 25:47

* * * * * * * *

He created man from crackling clay like the potters... *Sura* 17:13

* * * * * * * *

Allah's loving care does encompass and deliver us from dangers. He is the only protector, how can we then forget Him and run after things that are mere creatures of His world and shall perish? *Sura 6:61*

* * * * * * * *

In the daily pageants of nature: the dawn and the restful night, the sun, the moon, and the stars that guide the mariner in distant seas, the rain clouds pouring abundance and the fruits that delight the hearts of man, can you not read the signs of Allah? No vision can comprehend Him, yet He comprehends all. *Sura 6:96*

* * * * * * * *

Allah is to all people most surely full of kindness, most merciful. *Sura* 2:143

* * * * * * *

Truth only comes from Allah, and it remains truth however men might try to conceal it or throw doubts on it. *Sura* 2:147

* * * * * * *

Allah guides you to a path that is straight. *Sura* 2:213

* * * * * * *

It is not righteousness that turns your face East or West. But it is righteousness to believe in Allah and the Last Day, and the angels, and the Book, and the Messenger; to spend of your substance out of love for Him, for your kin, for orphans, for the needy, for the wayfarer, and for those who ask, and for the ransom of slaves; to be steadfast in prayer, and practice regular charity, to fulfill the contracts which you have made and to be firm and patient in pain or suffering and adversity, and through periods of panic. Such are the people of truth, the God-fearing. *Sura* 2:213

* * * * * * *

In the changing, fleeting world, His word is always true, and will remain through all the ages ever the same. (Quran, p. 1722)

* * * * * * *

He will see the ordered Plan of God. To Him must he return and give account! Let him then learn his lessons and live! (Quran, p. 1726)

* * * * * * *

Allah's guidance is ever nigh, if man will choose it. (Quran p.1745)

134

* * * * * * *

He was content and consoled in the thought that Allah has bestowed His loving care on him in the past, and so the future was sure. He followed the light divine. (Quran p. 1750)

* * * * * * *

He must strive at every stage and look to God alone as the goal of all his hopes. (Quran p. 1754)

* * * * * * *

The temporary relationships, the fleeting events, our triumphs, defeats and difficulties in this phenomenal world are the bridges through which we pass to the higher world. Our temporal experiences are the foundation on which our greater and real life is built. (Quran p.592)

* * * * * * *

Blessed indeed is the Night of Power when the mercy of Allah's revelation breaks through the darkness of the human soul! All the powers of the world divine speed on their mystic message of mercy by Allah's command and bless every nook and corner of the heart. (Quran, p. 1764)

* * * * * * *

A Balance of Justice will weigh and appraise all deeds. (Quran p. 1776)

* * * * * * *

Time is always in favor of those who have faith, live clean and pure lives, and know how to wait in patience and constancy. (Quran p. 1782)

* * * * * * *

Waste not nor misuse your life. Time through the ages bears witness that nothing remains but faith and good deeds, and the teaching of truth and the teaching of patience and constancy. But for these, man against time is in loss! (Quran p. 1782)

* * * * * * *

Faith is not a matter of words, but of *accepting* Allah's will. (Quran p.1402)

* * * * * * *

All acts of men must have their inevitable fruits. (Quran p. 1431)

* * * * * * *

It is not for us to justify ourselves, but to offer ourselves as we are. (Quran p. 1442)

* * * * * * * *

He knows you well when He brings you out of the earth and when you are hidden in your mother's wombs, therefore justify not yourself. *Sura* 53:32

* * * * * * *

In His hands are laughter and tears, life and death, the mystery of birth and creation and the hereafter. He controls our bliss and inner satisfaction. He is Lord of the highest and noblest in nature. His hand traces the course of history. Learn, oh learn for His revelation, and adore the Lord of your inmost Soul! (Quran p. 1448)

* * * * * * *

Death and his twin brother sleep are in the hands of Allah, to Him is our goal. (Quran p. 1243)

136

* * * * * * * *

Despair not of the mercy of Allah, for Allah forgives all sins for He is oft-forgiving, most merciful. *Sura* 39:53

* * * * * * *

The prayer of those without faith is nothing but futile wandering in mazes of error. *Sura* 40:50

* * * * * * *

Man does not weary of asking for good things, but if ill touches him he gives up hope and is lost in despair. *Sura* 41:47

* * * * * * *

No date-fruit comes out of its sheath, nor does female conceive in her womb, not bring forth young but by His knowledge. *Sura* 41:47

* * * * * * *

He sends inspiration to you as He did to those before you. Allah exalted in power, full of wisdom.

* * * * * * *

Consider the signs of Allah's gracious kindness around you and glorify Him. (Quran p. 1323)

* * * * * * *

What we call the ills of life are due to our own ill-deeds, and many of them are forgiven by Allah. His Plan can never be frustrated. This life is but a stage of convenience: live true and resist all wrong, but learn the best way to do so. On Allah rely, else no protector will you find. Allah's revelation comes as a guide and mercy; it shows the straight way, the way of Allah all-wise. (Quran p. 1314)

* * * * * * * *

He has made for you the earth as a carpet spread out, and has made for you roads and channels therein, in order that you may find guidance on the way. *Sura* 43:10

* * * * * * * *

Spiritual worth is measured by other things than gold or silver or the adornments of this world. (Quran p. 1329)

* * * * * * * *

The future is sure and in the hands of Allah to whom all will bend the knee. (Quran p. 1354)

* * * * * * * *

He will remove from them their ills and improve their condition. *Sura* 47:2

* * * * * * * *

Allah is with you and will never put you in loss for your good deeds. *Sura* 47:35

* * * * * * * *

The life of this world is but play and amusement. *Sura* 47:36

* * * * * * * *

Allah may forgive you your faults of the past and those to follow; fulfill His favor to you that He may guide you along the straight way. *Sura* 48:2

* * * * * * * *

They say with their tongues what is not in their hearts. *Sura* 48:11

* * * * * * * *

God's Plan works unceasingly. (Quran p. 945)

* * * * * * * *

Allah guides whom He will; He knows best those who receive guidance. *Sura* 28:56

* * * * * * * *

Do good as Allah has been good to you! *Sura 28:77*

* * * * * * * *

Everything that exists will perish except His own face. *Sura* 28:88

* * * * * * * *

Wealth is for service, not for hoarding or show. (Quran p.1023)

* * * * * * * *

The strength and skill, the beauty and power, of this world's life are no more than a spider's web – flimsy before the force of eternal truths that flow from Allah supreme. (Quran p. 1035)

* * * * * * * *

True wisdom sees Allah's boundless bounties to man, and how all nature is made to serve man's ends. It is due from us to know our place, to discern the limits of our knowledge, and see how far above us is Allah's wisdom and law. Let us not deceive ourselves. The end of all things will come, but the when and how are known to Allah alone, to whom be all praise. (Quran p. 1085)

* * * * * * *

So put your trust in God; for you are on the path of truth. *Sura* 27:79

* * * * * * *

Nor does anyone know what it is that he will earn on the morrow; nor does he know in what land he is to die. Verily with Allah is full knowledge and He is acquainted with all things. *Sura* 31:34

* * * * * * *

What counts is the intention of your heart. *Sura* 33:43

* * * * * * *

Learn then that the mercy and power, wisdom and justice of Allah are beyond all comparison: do right and prepare for the final day. (Quran p. 1132)

* * * * * * *

He it is who sends blessings on you, as do His angels, that He may bring you out from the depths of Darkness into Light. *Sura* 33:43

* * * * * * *

Man can see by his experience what infinite shades and grades of color there are in nature. So are their grades in the spiritual world. The good

140

and the true understand Allah who knows and watches over all His creatures. (Quran p. 1160)

* * * * * * * *

It is He who hears all things and is ever near. *Sura* 34:50

* * * * * * * *

Allah is free of all needs; it is we who need Him. Let us seek His love and live! (Quran p. 1151)

* * * * * * * *

Allah has, out of His bounty, settled us in a home that will last; no toil nor sense of weariness shall touch us there. *Sura* 35:35

* * * * * * * *

He forgives again and again. *Sura* 39:5

* * * * * * * *

Your Lord knows best what is in your hearts. *Sura* 17:25

* * * * * * * *

Faith is a refuge in ways we know not; time itself works Allah's plans before we know how it passes; He can give us rest and raise us back to life against all odds. (Quran p.727)

* * * * * * * *

Nor say of anything: 'I shall be sure to do so-and-so tomorrow,' without adding: 'so please God' (*Inshallah*) Sura *18:44*

* * * * * * * *

Good deeds are the best possessions in Allah's sight. *Sura* 18:46

* * * * * * * *

In human affairs many things are inexplicable, which are the things of the highest wisdom in the Universal Plan. (Quran p. 747)

* * * * * * *

I cast the garment of love over you. *Sura* 20:9

* * * * * * * *

The good things of this life may make a brave show, but they are nothing compared with the good in the hereafter. Both are provided by Allah. *Sura 20: 131*

* * * * * * * *

It is Allah who calls because He cares for you! (Quran p. 828)

* * * * * * * *

No good deed is fruitless; work while yet there is time. *Sura* 21:94

* * * * * * * *

Serve Allah humbly and He will protect and help you. (Quran p. 848)

* * * * * * * *

Allah is the light of the heavens and the earth, high above our petty evanescent lives; He illumines our souls with means that reach our inmost being. (Quran p. 139)

* * * * * * * *

142

You may not know, but Allah does know the inwardness of things both great and small. (Quran p. 915)

* * * * * * * *

Slowly Allah's revelation comes in ways most conducive to man's enlightenment. Men in their folly reject the most obvious signs of Allah. (Quran p. 931)

* * * * * * * *

The world of visible beauty is but the screen of the invisible and ineffable beauty within. (Quran p.597)

* * * * * * * *

Plot or plan as man will; it is Allah's will that must prevail. (Quran p. 601)

* * * * * * * *

Allah will never change the condition of a people until they change it themselves. *Sura* 13:14

* * * * * * * *

Revelation leads mankind from the depths of darkness into light. It comes to every age and nation in its own language. *Sura* 14:1

* * * * * * * *

His will and plan may be above comprehension, but will prevail over all things. It is not like the will of man, who may plan good things but is not necessarily able to carry them out. *Sura* 14:34

* * * * * * * *

He gives you all that you ask for. But if you count the favors of Allah, never will you be able to number them. *Sura* 14:34

* * * * * * * *

Let us be gentle and kind, and adore and serve our Lord all our lives. (Quran p. 651)

* * * * * * * *

Overlook any human faults with gracious forgiveness. *Sura* 15:25

* * * * * * * *

Lower your wings in gentleness to the believers. *Sura* 15:88

* * * * * * * *

Serve your Lord until there comes to you the hour that is certain. *Sura* 15:99

* * * * * * * *

He gave you hearing and sight and intelligence and affections that you may give thanks. *Sura* 16:78

* * * * * * * *

Allah's truth may come in stages, but it gives strength, guidance and glad tiding, and should be held fast when once received. *Sura* 16:101

* * * * * * * *

Allah's gifts are for all, but not all receive the same gifts, nor are all gifts of equal dignity or excellence. *Sura* 17:21

* * * * * * * *

It is not for us to question Allah's plan, which is full of wisdom and mercy for all. *Sura* 3:129

* * * * * * *

When we feel depressed at the chances and changes of time, we forget that the eternal God lives and watches over us and over all His creatures now as in all history in the past and in the future. *Sura* 3:144

* * * * * * *

It is want of faith that makes people afraid. *Sura* 3:156

* * * * * * *

When you have taken a decision, put your trust in God. Allah loves those who put their trust in Him. *Sura* 3:159

* * * * * * *

All gifts are ours in trust only. *Sura 3:180*

* * * * * * *

Oh you who believe! Persevere in patience and constancy, strengthen each other and fear Allah that you may prosper. *Sura* 3:200

* * * * * * *

Fight the good fight, and never fear, for this life is short and the hereafter eternal. *Sura* 4:74

* * * * * * *

What wonderful destiny is yours! Created to be Allah's vicegerent on earth! A little higher than the angels! *Sura* 2:30

* * * * * * * *

Our hearts are the wrappings which preserve God's word: we need no more. *Sura* 2:88

* * * * * * * *

His ways are wondrous and they are clear to those who have faith. *Sura* 2:87

* * * * * * * *

Whoever submits his whole self to Allah and is a doer of good, he will get his reward with his Lord; on such shall be no fear, nor shall they grieve. *Sura* 2:112

* * * * * * * *

Islam meant the willing submission of his will to Allah; the active attainment of Peace through conflict. (Quran p.11)

* * * * * * * *

Righteousness does not consist of formalities, but in faith, kindness, prayer, charity, probity, and patience with suffering. (Quran p. 16)

* * * * * * * *

Life is movement, activity, striving, fighting against baser things. (Quran p. 16)

* * * * * * * *

We have sent down to you manifest signs (*ayat*) Sura 2:97

* * * * * * * *

We must never forget our own personal responsibility for what we do, or deceive ourselves by the illusion of vicarious atonement. *Sura* 6:70

* * * * * * *

The life of this world is but empty; what is serious is the life hereafter. Allah's wisdom pervades the whole of His creation, and in His hands are the keys to the unseen, and the secrets of all that we see. *Sura* 6:32

* * * * * * *

To God belongs the East and the West: wherever you turn, there is the Presence of God. *Sura* 2:115

* * * * * * *

To each is a goal to which Allah turns him   *Sura* 2:148

* * * * * * *

We offer ourselves to Allah and seek His light. (Quran p.13)

* * * * * * *

Kind words and the covering of faults are better than charity followed by injury. *Sura* 2:263

* * * * * * *

Cancel not your charity by reminders of your generosity or by injury, like those who spend their substance to be seen of men. *Sura 2:264*

* * * * * * *

In your hands is all good. *Sura* 3:26

* * * * * * *

When we submit to Allah's will, the real Islam illuminates us. *Sura 3:26*

* * * * * * *

It is unselfishness that Allah demands, and there is not an act of unselfishness, however small or intangible, but is well within the knowledge of Allah. Give freely of that which you love. *Sura 3:92*

* * * * * * *

And the unbelievers plotted and planned and the best of planners is God. *Sura 3:54*

* * * * * * *

And if anyone obeys his own impulse to do good, be sure that Allah is He who recognizes and knows. *Sura 2:158*

* * * * * * * *

Man's power is nothing; his faith should be in Allah. *Sura 2:257*

* * * * * * *

Fighting is prescribed for you, and you dislike it, but it is possible that you dislike a thing which is good for you, and you love a thing which is bad for you. Allah knows. *Sura 2*

* * * * * * *

Allah will not call you to account for thoughtlessness in your oaths, but for the intention of your hearts, and He is forgiving and most forbearing. *Sura 2:225*

* * * * * * *

Life and Death are in the hands of Allah

Allah's plan is universal, and He carries it out as He wills. *Sura 2:243*

* * * * * * *

God cares for all and He knows all things. *Sura 2:248*

* * * * * * *

Allah is with those who steadfastly persevere. *Sura 2:249*

* * * * * *

Spend out of the bounties we have provided for you. *Sura 2:254*

* * * * * *

Let there be no compulsion in religion; truth stands out clear from error; whoever rejects evil and believes in God has grasped the most trustworthy handhold that never breaks. God hears and knows all things. *Sura 2:256*

* * * * * * *

Man's power is nothing; his faith should be in Allah. *Sura 2:257*

* * * * * * *

God will give light according to His wisdom. *Sura 2:272*

* * * * * * *

All our life in this world must be lived as in the presence of Allah. The finest example of faith we have is in the Apostle's life: full of faith, let us render willing obedience to Allah's will. Our responsibility, though great, is not a burden greater than we can bear, let us pray for Allah's assistance and He will help. *Sura 2:284*

* * * * * * * *

To Allah is the end of all journeys. *Sura 2:285*

* * * * * * * *

On no soul does God place a burden greater than it can bear. *Sura 2:286*

* * * * * * * *

Allah never fails in His promise. *Sura 3:9*

* * * * * * * *

The nearness to Allah is the best of all goals. *Sura 3:14*

* * * * * * * *

When we submit to Allah's will, the real Islam illuminates us. *Sura 3:28*

* * * * * * * *

Whatever you hide in your hearts or reveal, Allah knows it all. He knows what is in the Heavens and what is on earth. And Allah has power over all things. *Sura 3:29*

* * * * * * * *

God provides sustenance to whom He pleases without measure. *Sura 3:37*

* * * * * * * *

And the unbelievers plotted and planned, and God too planned, and the best of planners is God. *Sura 3:54*

* * * * * * * *

150

Whoever holds firmly to God will be shown a way that is straight. *Sura 3:101*

* * * * * * *

So lose not heart nor fall into despair, for you must gain mastery if you are true in faith. *Sura 3:139*

* * * * * * *

He is the best disposer of affairs. *Sura 3:173*

* * * * * * *

Our duty is to hold fast by faith and lead a good life. *Sura 3:179*

* * * * * * *

The essence of Islam is to serve Allah and do good to your fellow creatures. *Sura 4:36*

* * * * * * *

Indeed God is never unjust even by the weight of an atom, and if one does a good deed, God will multiply it and give from Him a great reward. *Sura 4:40*

* * * * * * *

Fight the good fight, and never fear, for this life is short and the hereafter eternal. *Sura 4:74*

* * * * * * *

Allah blots out sins and forgives again and again. *Sura 4:99*

* * * * * * *

But recognize with justice those who are sincere and humble, though they themselves be not of your flock, if they witness to Truth. *Sura 4:47*

* * * * * * * *

The goal of you all is to Allah; it is He that will show you the truth of the matter in which you dispute. *Sura 4:51*

* * * * * * * *

There is not a good deed which you do, but God is well-acquainted therewith. *Sura 4:127*

* * * * * * * *

We realize His love in loving and doing good to His creatures, and our love for Him is meaningless without such good. *Sura 5:96*

* * * * * * * *

God forgive us what is past. *Sura 5:98*

* * * * * * * *

God knows all that you reveal and conceal. *Sura 5:102*

* * * * * * * *

Jesus did feed his disciples by miracle, but he claimed not divinity; he was a true servant of Allah. *Sura 5:119*

* * * * * * * *

He is it who created you from clay, and then decreed a stated term for you. He knows what you hide and what you reveal, and He knows the recompense you earn by your deeds. *Sura 6:2*

152

* * * * * * * *

He knows the secret whisper and what is yet more hidden; with Him are the keys of the unseen. *Sura 6:12*

* * * * * * * *

If Allah touches you with affliction, none can remove it but He; if He touches you with happiness, He has power over all things. *Sura 6:17*

* * * * * * * *

The life of this world is but empty; what is the life hereafter, Allah's wisdom pervades the whole of His creation, and in His hands are the keys of the unseen. And the secrets of all that we see. *Sura 6:32*

* * * * * * * *

I follow what is revealed to me. *Sura 6:51*

* * * * * * * *

There is no grain in the darkness or depths of the earth, not anything fresh or dry, green or withered, but is inscribed in the Record clear to those who can read. *Sura 6:59*

* * * * * * * *

In the end to Him will be your return; then He will show you the truth of all you did. *Sura 6:60*

* * * * * * * *

He is Allah, your lord! There is no god but He, the creator of all things. Worship Him and He has power to dispose of all things. *Sura 6:102*

* * * * * * * *

There are signs given by Allah everyday, understood by those who believe. *Sura 6:109*

* * * * * * * *

Those whom Allah (in His Plan) wills to guide, He opens their breast to Islam. *Sura 6:125*

* * * * * * * *

Our duty is to maintain unity and discipline and do the duty that comes to us. *Sura 6:164*

* * * * * * * *

For them will be a home of peace in the presence of their Lord; He will be their Friend, because they practiced righteousness. *Sura 6:152*

* * * * * * * *

Our God can reach out to the utmost reaches of things with His knowledge. *Sura 7:89*

* * * * * * * *

We vow we shall ever be grateful. *Sura 7:189*

* * * * * * * *

And We shall remove from their hearts any lurking sense of injury. *Sura 7:43*

* * * * * * * *

Know that Allah comes in between a man and his heart. *Sura 8:20*

* * * * * * * *

154

Be sure that God is your protector, the best to protect and the best to help. *Sura 8:40*

* * * * * * * *

Wealth is for use and on trust for mankind; hoard not nor misuse it. *Sura 9:35*

* * * * * * * *

And He had put affection between their hearts, not if you had spent all that is in the earth could you have produced that affection. *Sura 8:63*

* * * * * * * *

Nothing will happen to us except what Allah has decreed for us. He is our protector and on Allah let the believers put their trust. *Sura 9:51*

* * * * * * * *

If God finds any good in your hearts, He will give you something better than what has been taken from you; and He will forgive you, for God is oft forgiving, most merciful. *Sura 8:70*

* * * * * * * *

O you who believe, fear God and be with those who are true in word and deed. *Sura 9:119*

* * * * * * * *

I have no power over any harm or profit to myself except as Allah wills. To every people is a term appointed. When our term is reached not an hour can they cause delay, nor an hour can they advance. *Sura 10:49*

* * * * * * * *

Allah's promise is assuredly true. *Sura 10:55*

* * * * * * * *

Oh Mankind! There has come to you a direction from your Lord and a healing for the disease of your hearts, and for those who believe guidance and mercy. *Sura 10:57*

* * * * * * * *

Be patient and strive with constancy and perseverance for all suffering and sorrow as well as all bounties proceed from Allah whose Plan is righteous and for the good of all His creatures. *Sura 10:109*

* * * * * * * *

Marvelous are God's mercies and strange are the ways of ungrateful men. *Sura 11:88*

* * * * * * * *

That which is left to you by Allah is best for you. *Sura 11:86*

* * * * * * * *

Allah is ever kind and His punishments are just. *Sura 11:108*

* * * * * * * *

And be steadfast in patience and Allah will not let the reward of the righteous to perish. *Sura 11:113*

* * * * * * * *

He bore his affliction with patience and faith in Allah. *Sura 12*

* * * * * * * *

Marked out by God for a destiny of greatness, righteousness, and benevolence. *Sura 12:6*

* * * * * * * *

So the story shows that the plan of Allah works without fail: it defeats the wiles of the wicked, turns evil to good, and ever leads those who are true to beatitudes undreamt of; will man not learn to rely on Allah as the only reality, turning away from all that is fleeting and untrue. *Sura 12:11*

* * * * * * * *

Every fact in life's grand pageant is but a portent of the future. Every soul is in pledge and must redeem itself by faith and prayer, by charity and earnest care of the realities of life. Bring but the will, and Allah will guide. (The Quran, p. 1639)

* * * * * * * *

Conscience bears witness that he must walk straight; for he must face that day's realities. With patience await the unfolding of Allah's wise purpose. Keep the hereafter in view. Think of Allah's purpose and the noble destiny for which Allah gave him life and its gifts. (The Holy Quran, p. 1648)

* * * * * * * *

Allah's grace flows freely: we have but to tune our will to His, the ever-loving, righteous Allah. (The Holy Quran, p.1692)

* * * * * * * *

But verily, over you are appointed angels to protect you. *Sura 62:10*

* * * * * * * *

Wonderful are the ways of Allah in creation, and the love with which He guides His creature's destinies, gives them means by which to strive for maturity by ordered steps, and reach the end most fitted for their natures. (The Holy Quran, p.1722)

Excerpts from <u>The Spirit of Islam</u> by Ameer Ali

A man once came to him with a bundle and said, 'O Prophet, I passed through a wood and heard the voice of the young birds, and I took them and put them in my carpet, and their mother came fluttering round my head.' And the Prophet said, 'Put them down.' And when he put them down the mother joined the young. And the Prophet said, 'Do you wonder at the affection of the mother towards her young? I swear by Him who has sent me, Verily, God is more loving to His servants than the mother to these young birds. Return them to the place from which you took them, and let their mother be with them.'

* * * * * * * *

'Fear God with regard to animals,' said Mohammad, 'ride them when they are fit to be ridden, and get off when they are tired. Verily, there are rewards for doing good to dumb animals, and giving them water to drink. (p. 157-158)

* * * * * * * *

These percepts of tenderness so lovingly embalmed in the creed and faithfully rendered into a common duty of everyday life is the world of Islam. (p. 158)

* * * * * * * *

Be constant in prayer and give alms, and what good you have sent before you for your souls shall find it with God. (p.151)

* * * * * * * *

Blessed is he who gives away his substance so he can become pure.
(p.151)

* * * * * * *

Quotes from Essential Sufism

The only peace comes from faith in God. (p. 171)

* * * * * * *

You can rely only on that which is truly healthy and whole, and that is God. (p. 171)

* * * * * * *

None of us knows how much time we have. (p.29)

* * * * * * *

The wise heart sees beyond the outer forms to inner reality. (p. 36)

* * * * * * *

So whatever you do, do it with love. *Sheik Muzaffer* p.55

* * * * * * *

Humility and self-awareness are among the prerequisites to wisdom. (p. 79)

* * * * * * *

If you wish to draw near to God, you must seek God in the hearts of others. You must speak well of all, whether present or absent. (p. 212)

* * * * * * *

If you do not walk toward Him, He comes to you running. *Mohammad* (p. 228)

* * * * * * *

Wherever you turn, there is the face of Allah. *Quran*

* * * * * * *

Die before you die. The wisdom we receive in death reveals the true value of what is important and what is not. (p. 252)

* * * * * * *

Indeed God has written a thousand promises all over your heart. *God's Bucket* (p/ 81)

* * * * * * *

Now is the season to know that everything you do is sacred. *Now is the Time* (p.161)

* * * * * * *

Know, O beloved, that man was not created in jest or at random, but marvelously made and for some great end. *Al Ghazzali* (p. 1)

* * * * * * *

I believe in God, and in God's angels, and in the Holy Books, and in God's messengers. And in the Day of Resurrection, and in destiny, that all good and bad come from God and that there is life after life. (p. 5-6)

* * * * * * *

162

Love is to see what is good and beautiful in everything. It is to learn from everything, to see the gifts of God and the generosity of God in everything. It is to be thankful for all God's bounties. (p.14)

* * * * * * * *

A much higher state is to be satisfied with whatever God provides for you, whether it mean comfort or discomfort, fulfillment of physical needs or not. (p. 20)

* * * * * * * *

A broken mirror creates a thousand reflections of a single image. If the mirror could be made whole again, it would then reflect the single, unified image. (p. 23)

* * * * * * * *

Thinking about one's own death is an exercise in becoming more aware of one's present experiences. (p. 28)

* * * * * * * *

The goal of self-transformation is to remove all the veils between us and God. (p.244)

* * * * * * * *

Quotes from Hafiz and Rumi

The wise man learns what draws God near. It is the beauty of compassion in your hearts.

* * * * * * *

All the talents of God are in you.

* * * * * * *

God has sent you a close one. He has seen your heart in prayer.

* * * * * * *

Something missing in my heart tonight has made my eyes so soft, my voice so tender, my need of God absolutely clear.

* * * * * * *

We have been *startled by God.*

* * * * * * *

I should not make any promises right now, but I know if you pray somewhere in this world something good will happen.

* * * * * * *

Your heart and my heart are very old friends.

* * * * * * *

Go running through the world giving love, giving love.

164

* * * * * * * *

Your wounds of love can only heal when you forgive this dream.

* * * * * * * *

Your life within God's arms, your dance within God's arms is already perfect.

* * * * * * * *

The sky where we live is no place to lose your wings. So love, love, love.

* * * * * * * *

A true saint is an earth in eternal Spring. *Rumi: Forgive the Dream* (p. 125)

* * * * * * * *

You have come into this world for a particular task, and that is your purpose. If you do not perform it, then you will have done nothing. *Rumi* (p. 214)

* * * * * * * *

Bibliography

Ali, Abdallah Yousef (translator), *The Glorious Kur'an with Translation and Commentary,* Beirut: Dar ElFikr.

Ali, Sayed Ameer Ali, *The Spirit of Islam*

Fadiman, James and Robert Frager (editors), *Essential Sufism,* San Francisco: HarperSanFrancisco, 1999.

Ladinsky, Daniel (translator,) *The Gift: Poems by Hafiz the Great Sufi Master,* New York: Penguin/Arkana, 1999.

Star, Jonathan (translator), *Rumi: In the Arms of the Beloved,* New York: Jeremy P. Tarcher/Putnam a member of Penguin Putnam Inc., 1997

www.ingramcontent.com/pod-product-compliance
Lightning Source LLC
Chambersburg PA
CBHW061722020426
42331CB00006B/1048